POLAR BEARS

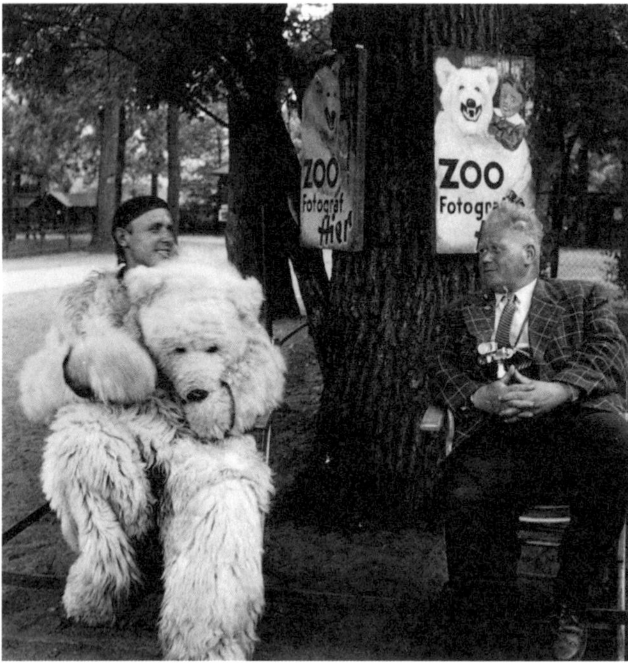
ZOO
Fotograf
hier
ZOO

POLAR BEARS

Jochen Raiß

HATJE
CANTZ

Preface

It is said that in times of climate change, the polar bear is the most popular animal in the world. In the 1920s, people presumably had less sympathy for it, but it was admired for its savage exoticism. It is not known who first came up with the idea of photographs of people posing with polar bears. A successful ad campaign by Steiff, the German manufacturer of stuffed animals, may have provided the inspiration, or maybe it was billboards for a large zoo. Jochen Raiß, the collector and editor of this book, considers both theses improbable. He believes some clever photographer at a seaside resort on the Baltic Sea must have been the first to discover polar bears as a business model, had his assistant get into a costume, and take photographs at popular tourist sites, which were then quickly developed by a second assistant.

Jochen Raiß works as a photo editor in Hamburg. He studied philosophy and German, and from an early age used black-and-white prints as bookmarks. He acquires his photographs at flea markets, and for nearly thirty years he has been collecting them and grouping them by motif, including "Women in Trees," "Women Sleeping Outdoors," and "Double Exposures." A book about the first group was published by Hatje Cantz in 2016.

The present collection is photographs of people posing with fake polar bears. He is interested in the care with which each group portrait was arranged. The sitters' shy gazes at the camera, which was not yet as familiar as it would become, their admiration for the imposing animal, whose dangerousness is merely suggested by its hide.

In the meantime, Raiß has some 2,500 to 3,000 prints, of which seventy-eight feature a polar bear; the earliest of them date from the 1920s, the last from the 1960s, by which time everyone could afford a camera, and black-and-white photographs were replaced by amateur color photographs—usually bad ones without any artistic value. These are German motifs: taken in Garmisch with the mountains in the background or on the shore at the Baltic Sea. Apparently, the polar bear never caught on in other countries.

Raiß has several colleagues who also hunt for anonymous photographs at flea markets, and the dealers have told him this. Photographs of polar bears—like early amateur photography in general—tend to be a male domain. Women were allowed to pose; that is their role. Women are often seen next to the polar bears, sometimes accompanied by their children. How often did the man absent in this photograph hide in his bear costume? In these photographs, it is left to the viewers' imagination to read from the images the stories that can reveal the constellation of the participants.

In any case, the collector Jochen Raiß has a lot of sympathy for all those sweaty anonymous people in polar bear costumes.

Norbert Thomma

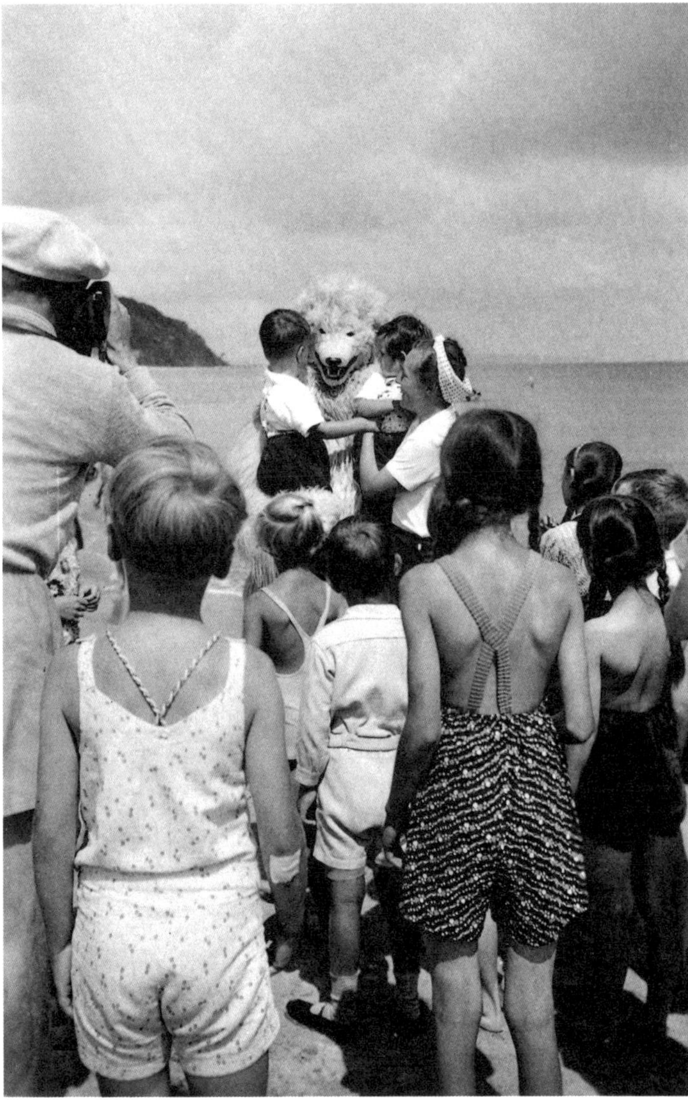

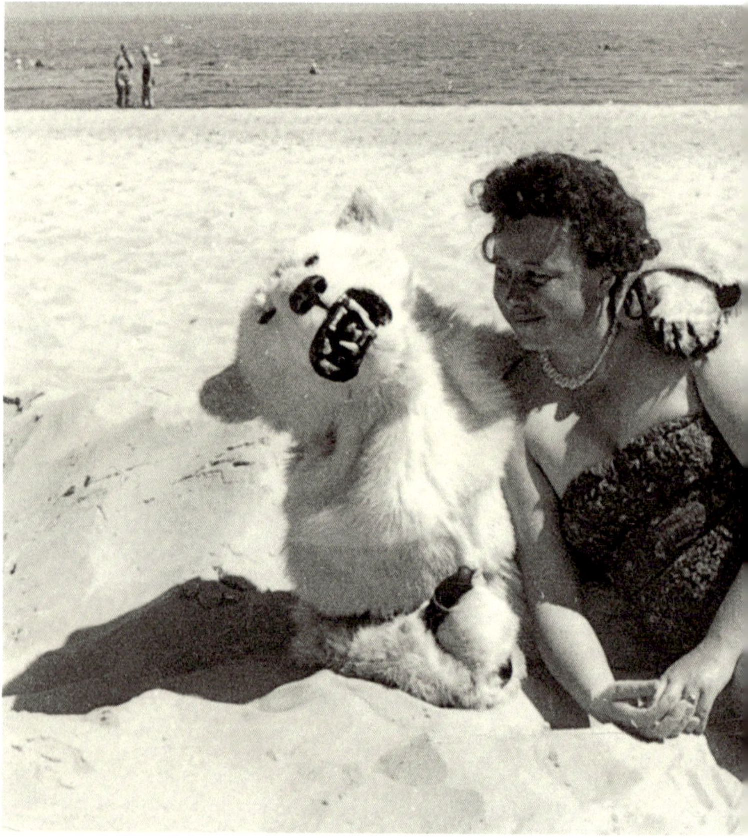

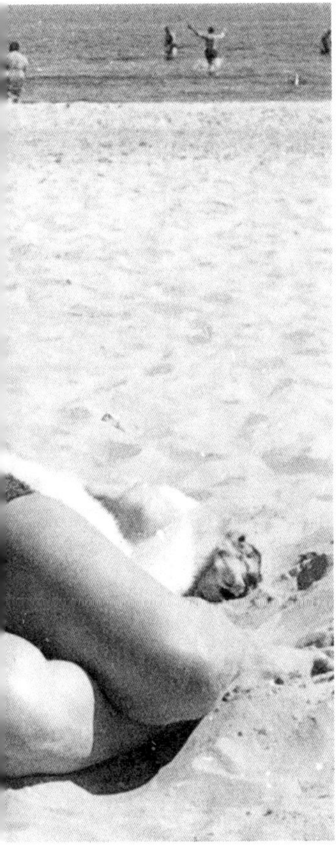

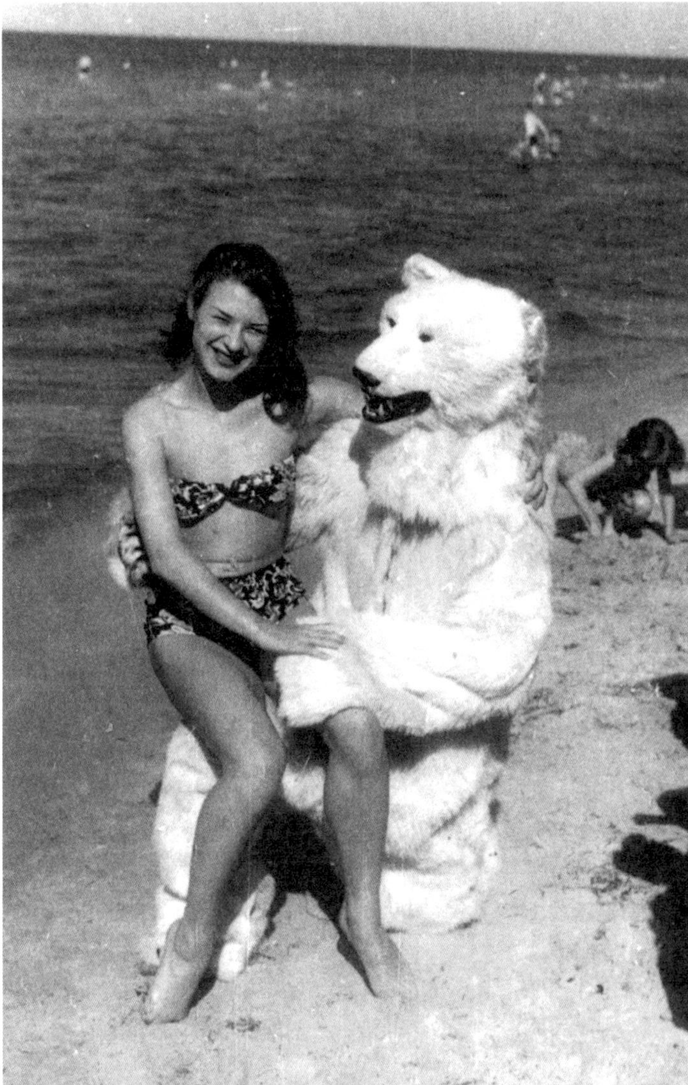

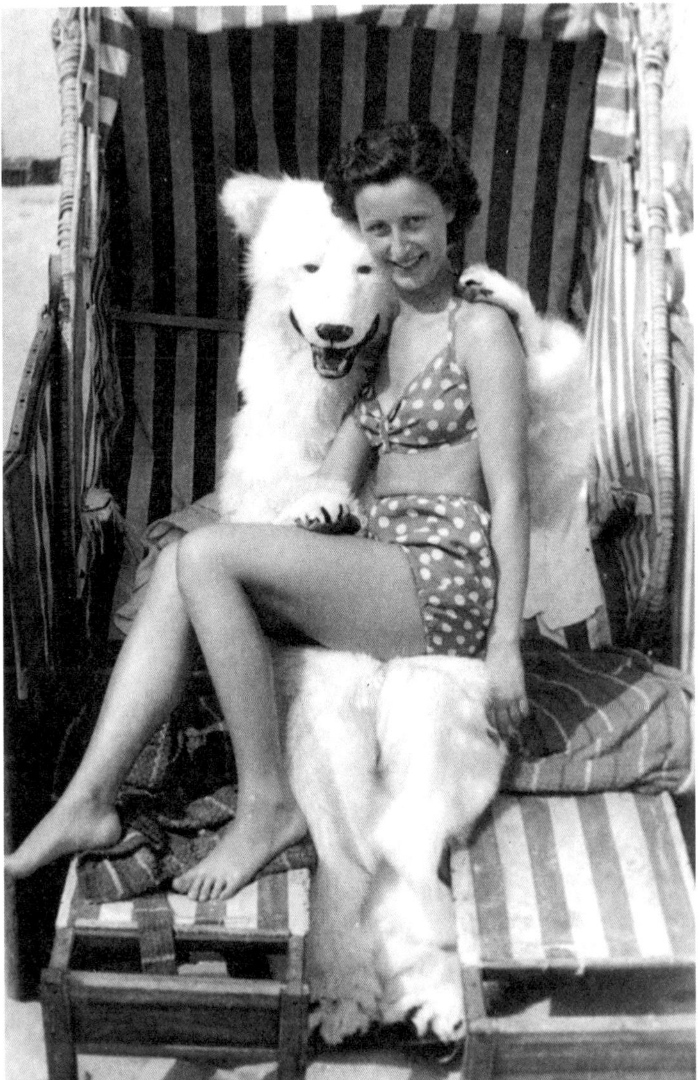

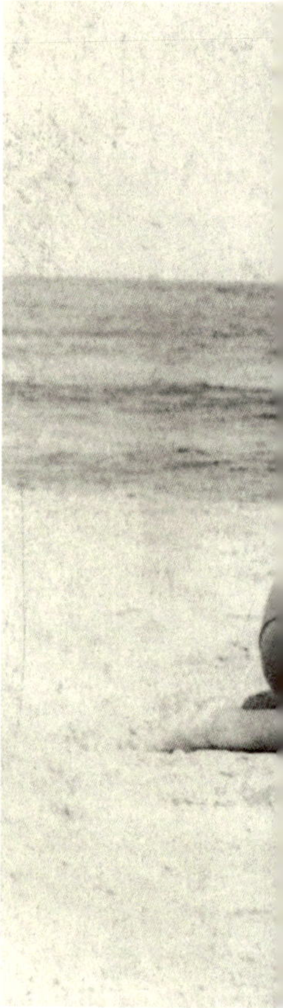

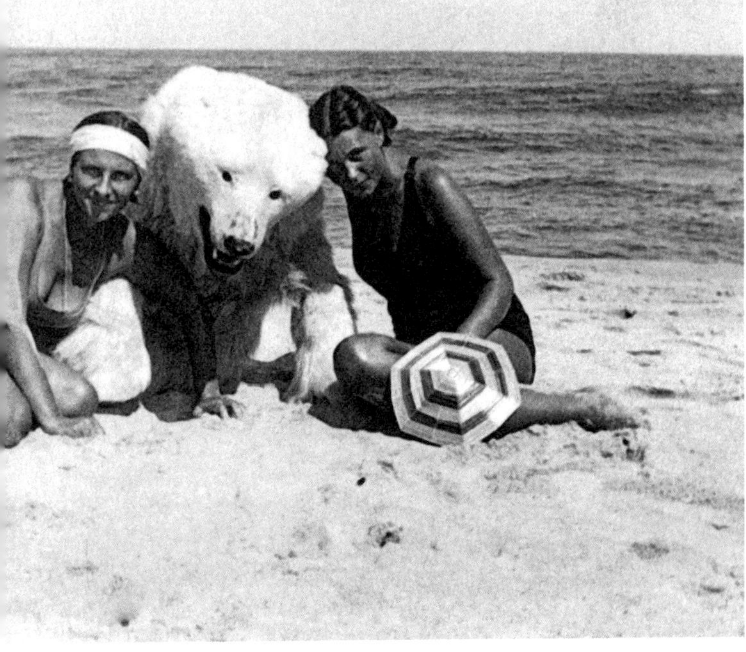

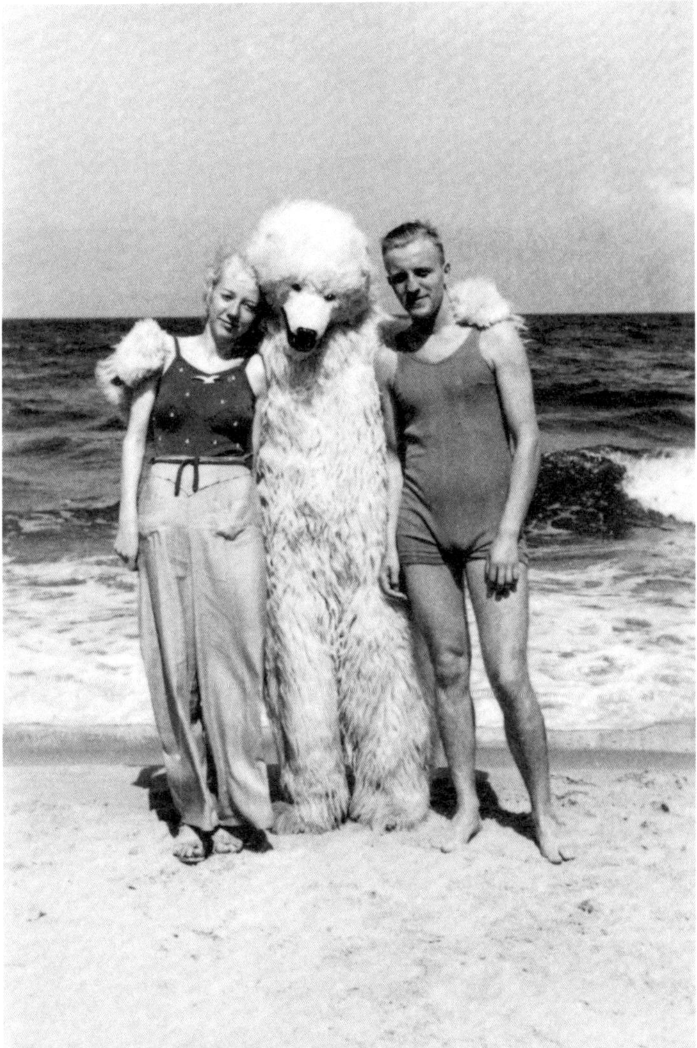

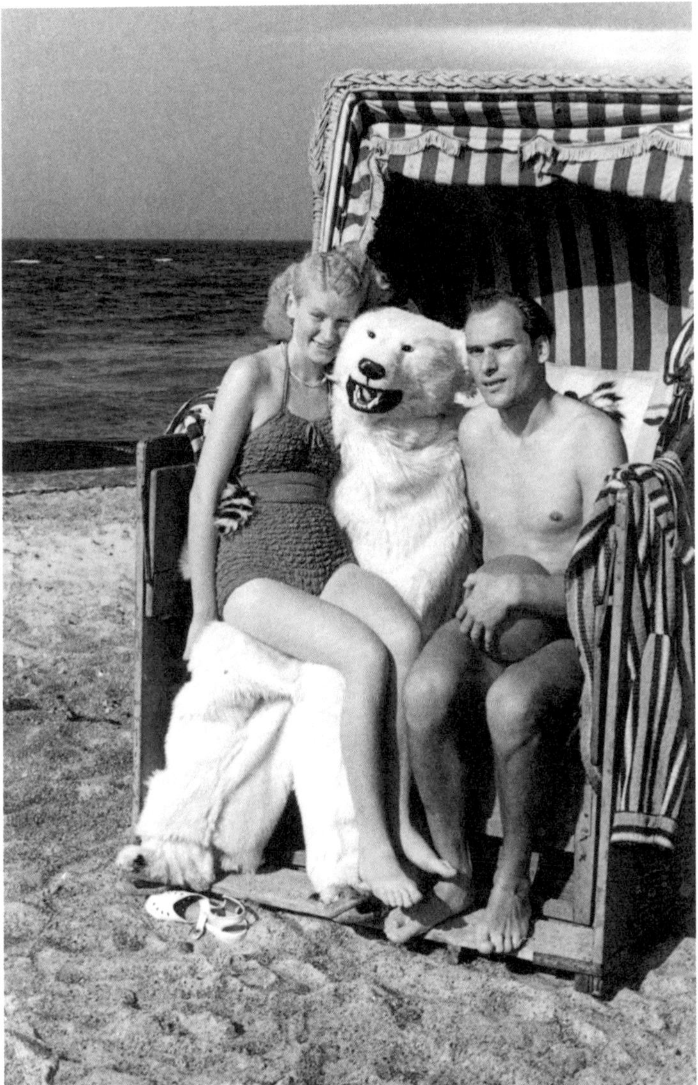

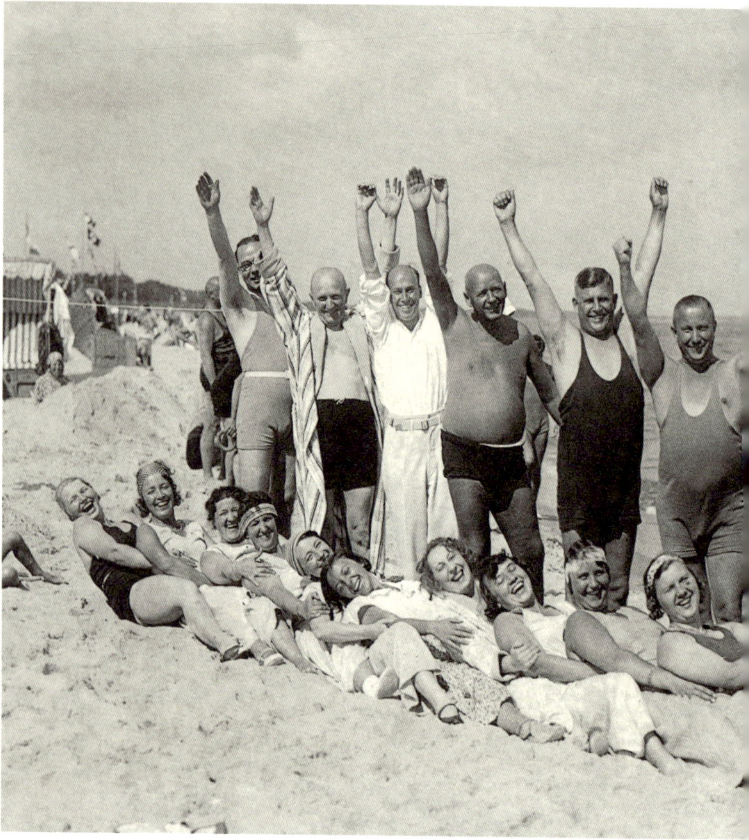

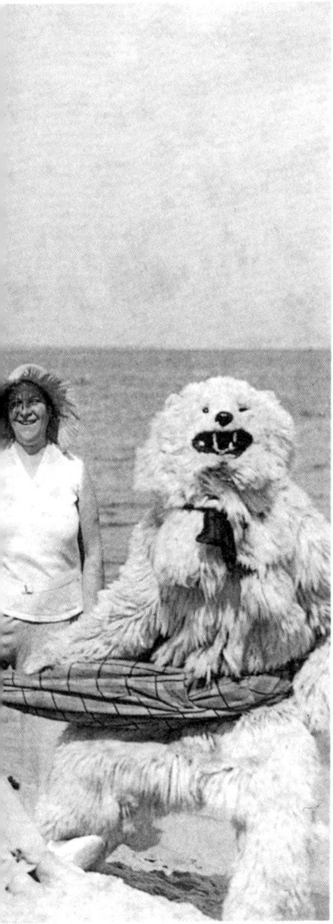

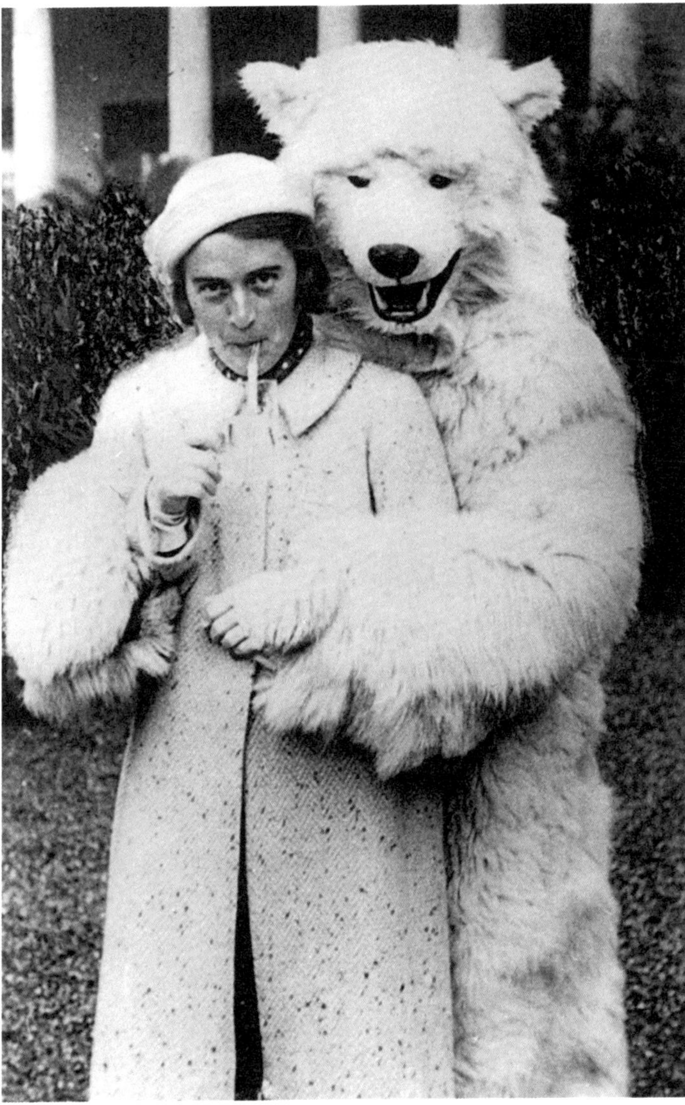

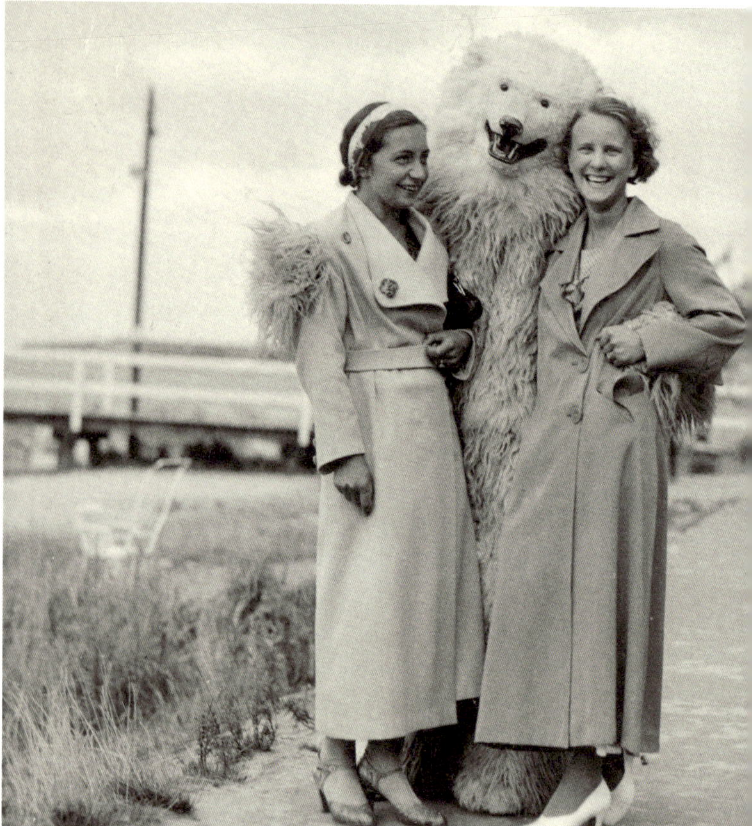

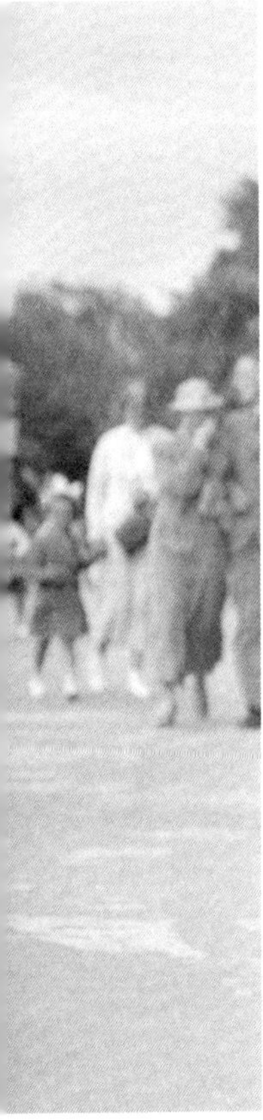

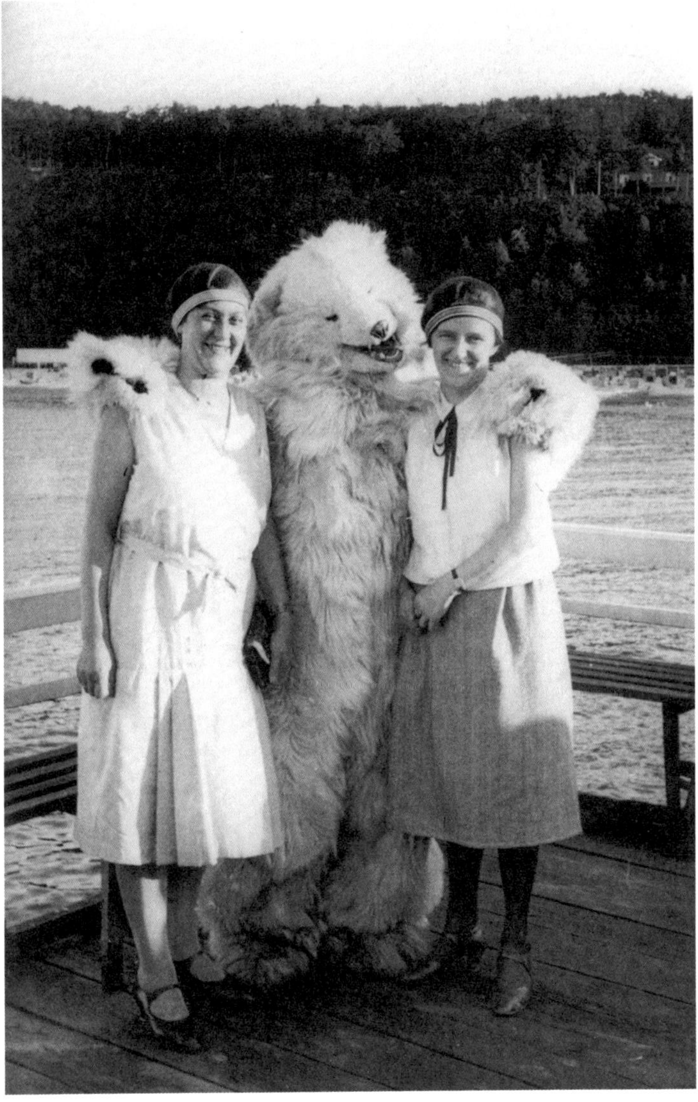

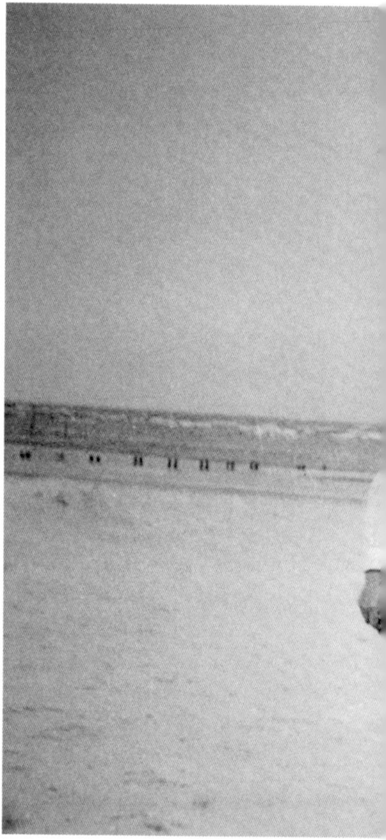

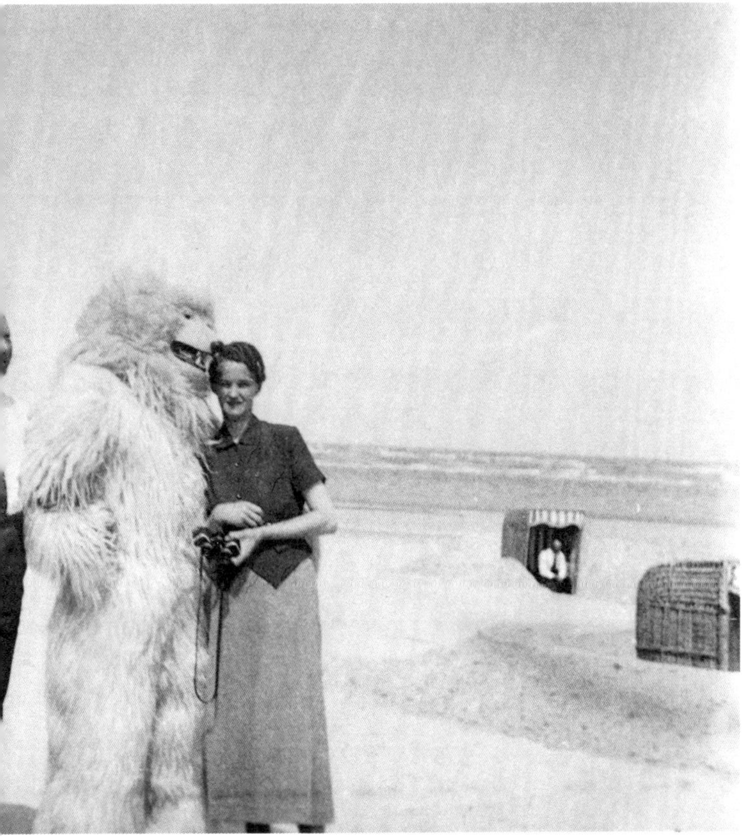

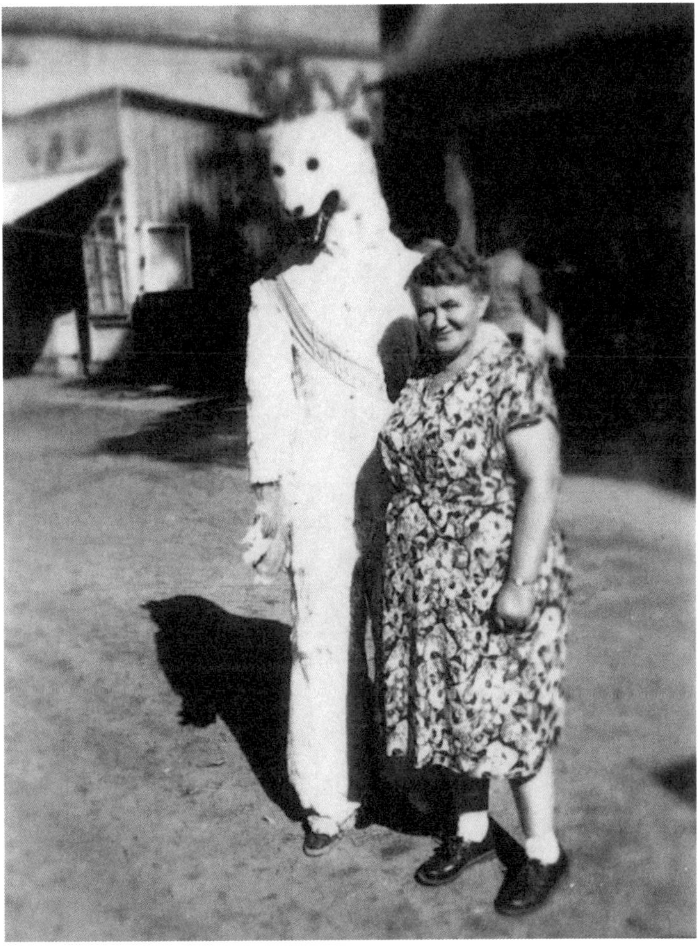

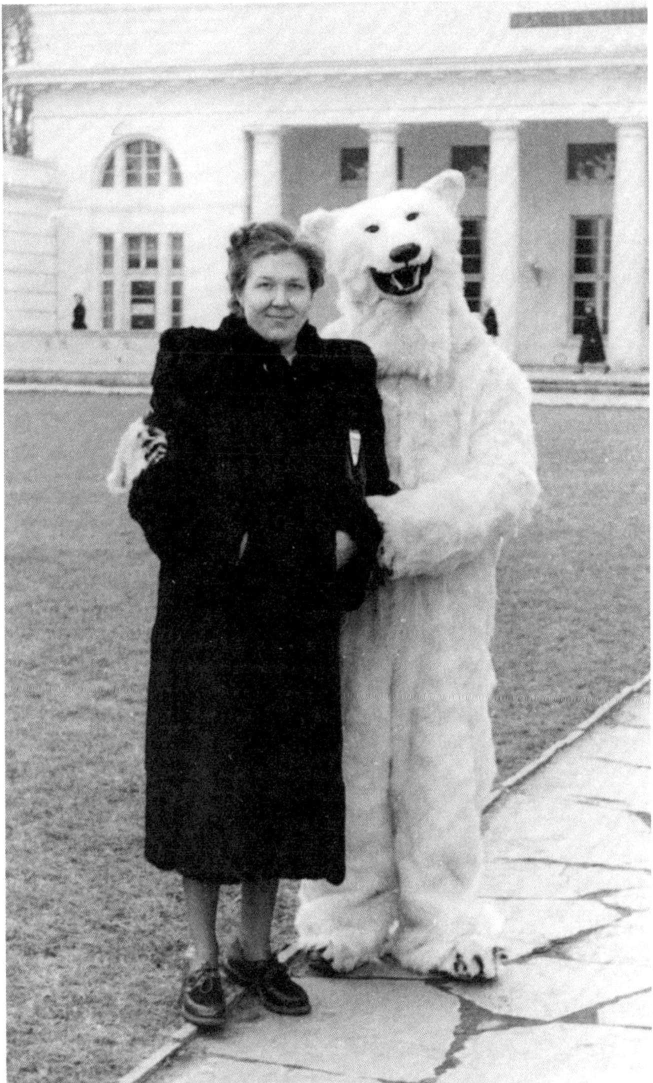

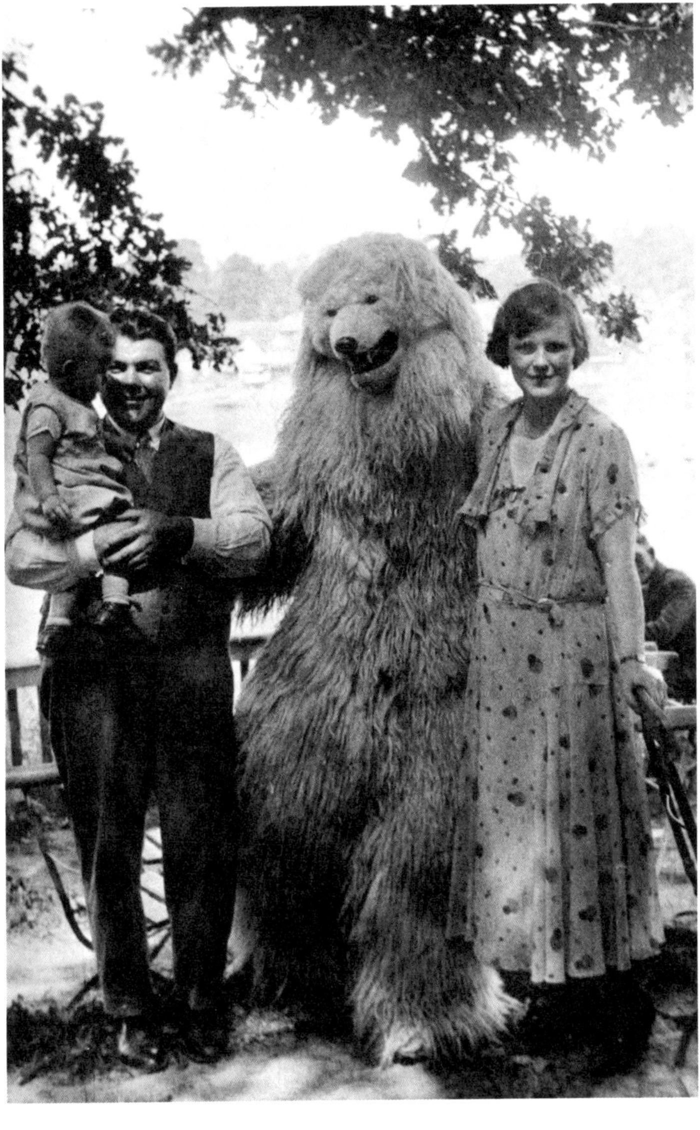

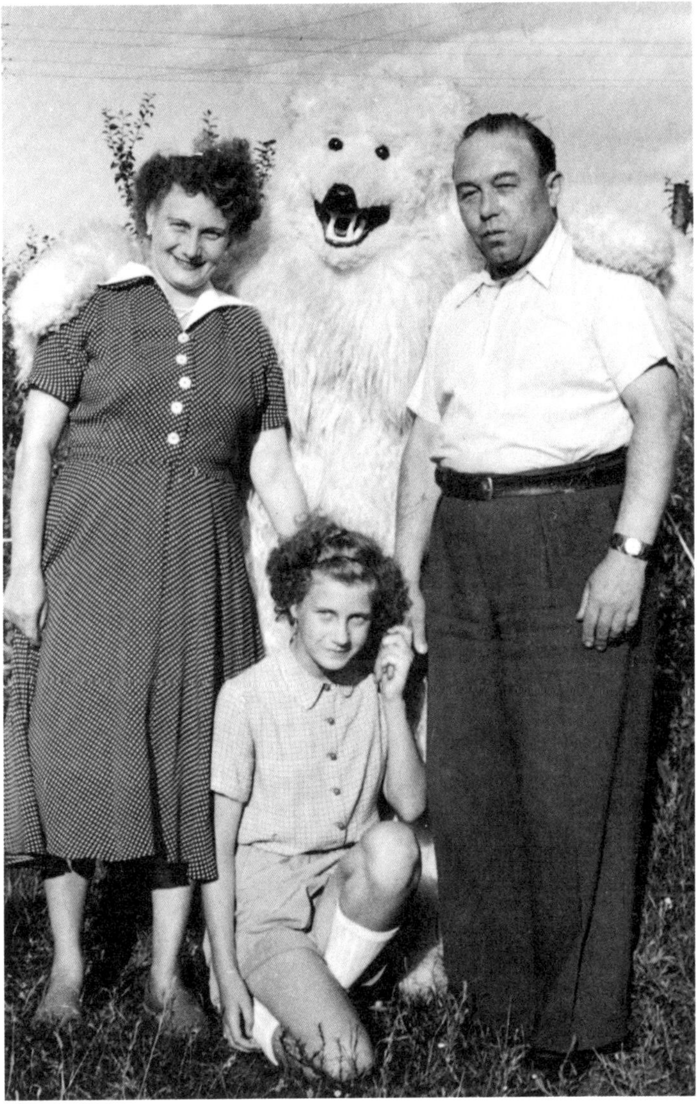

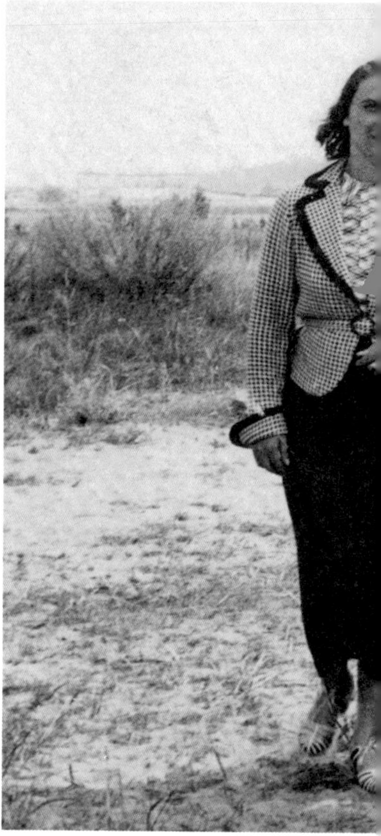

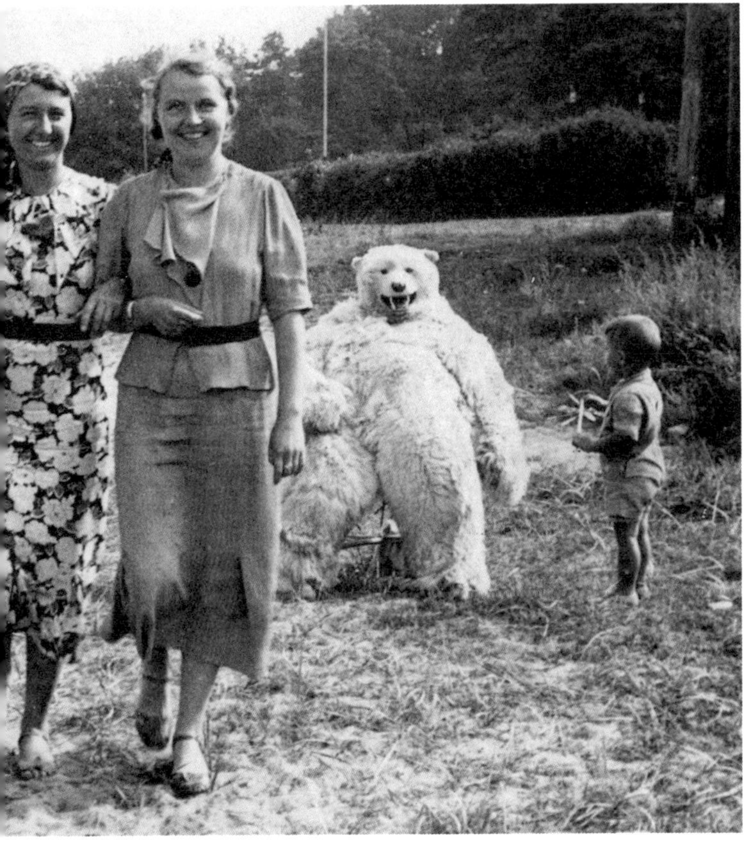

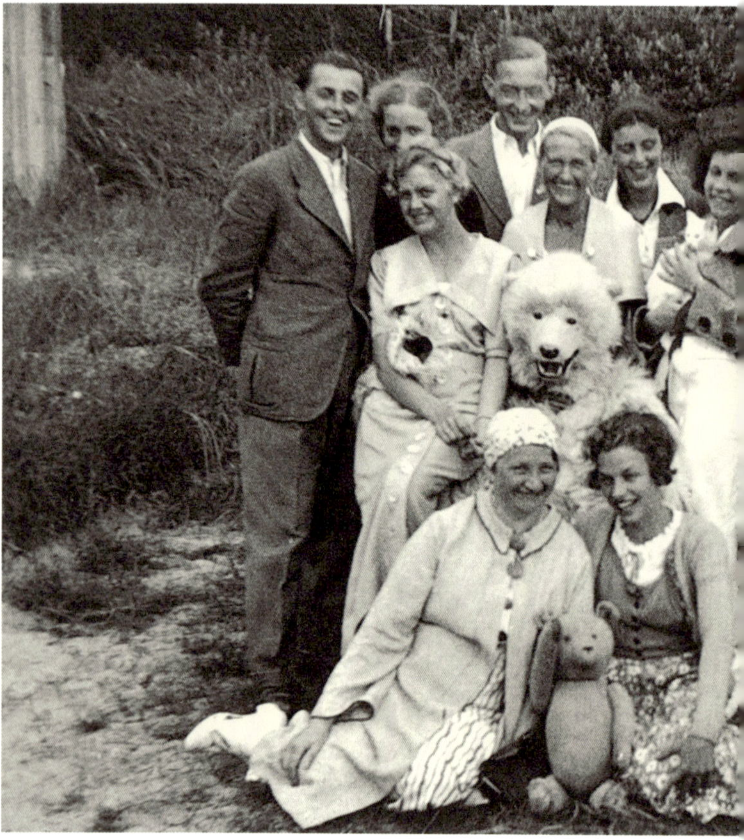

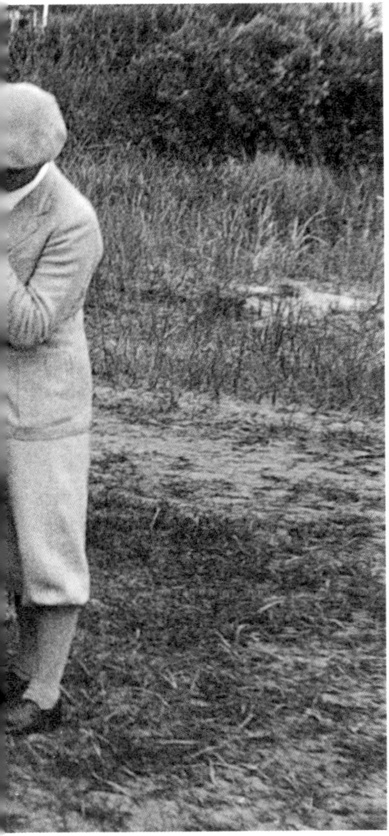

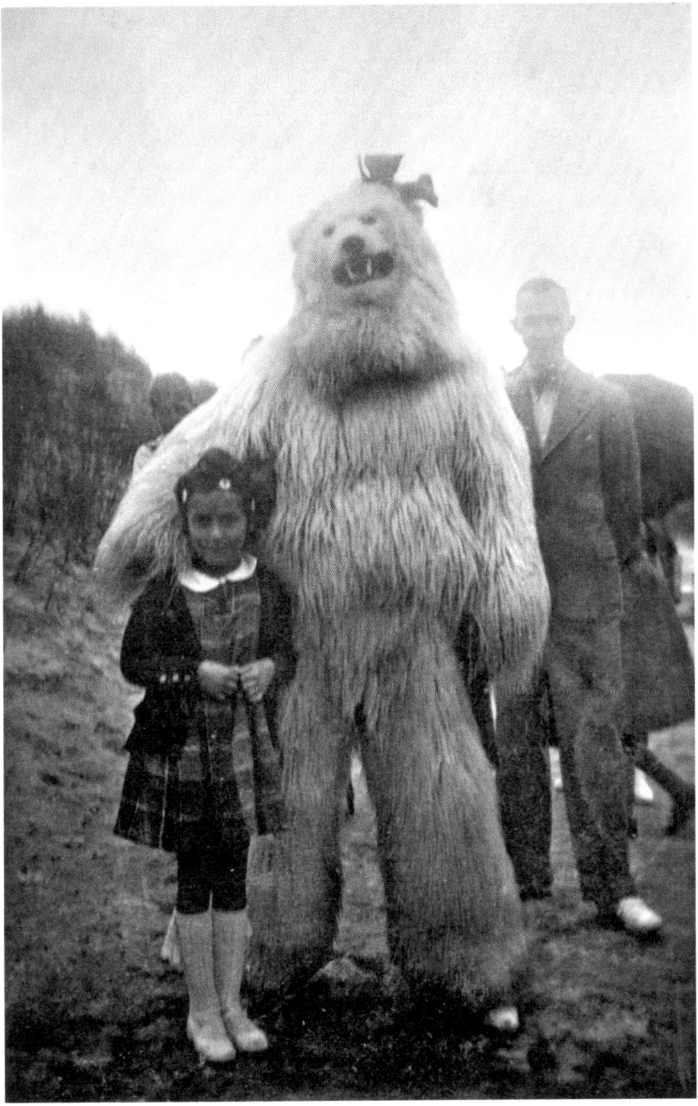

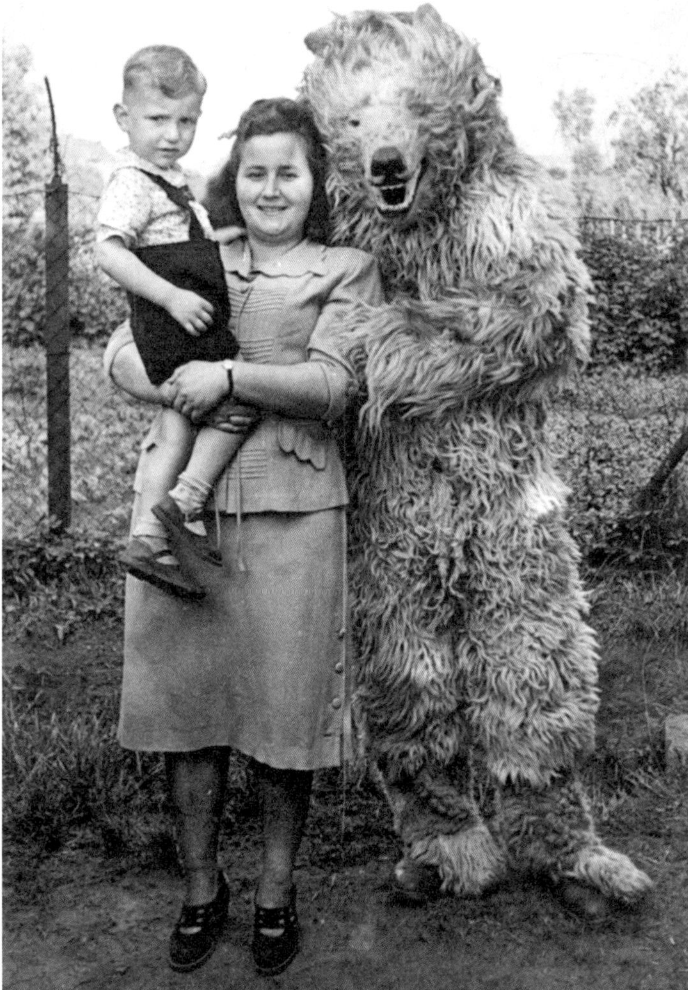

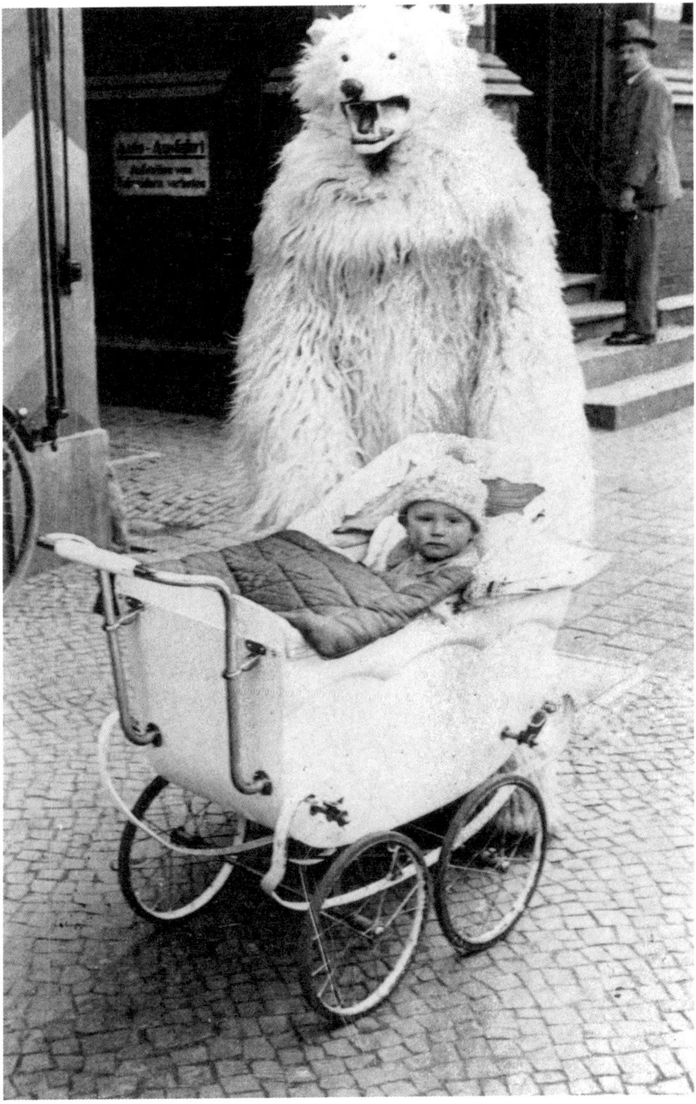

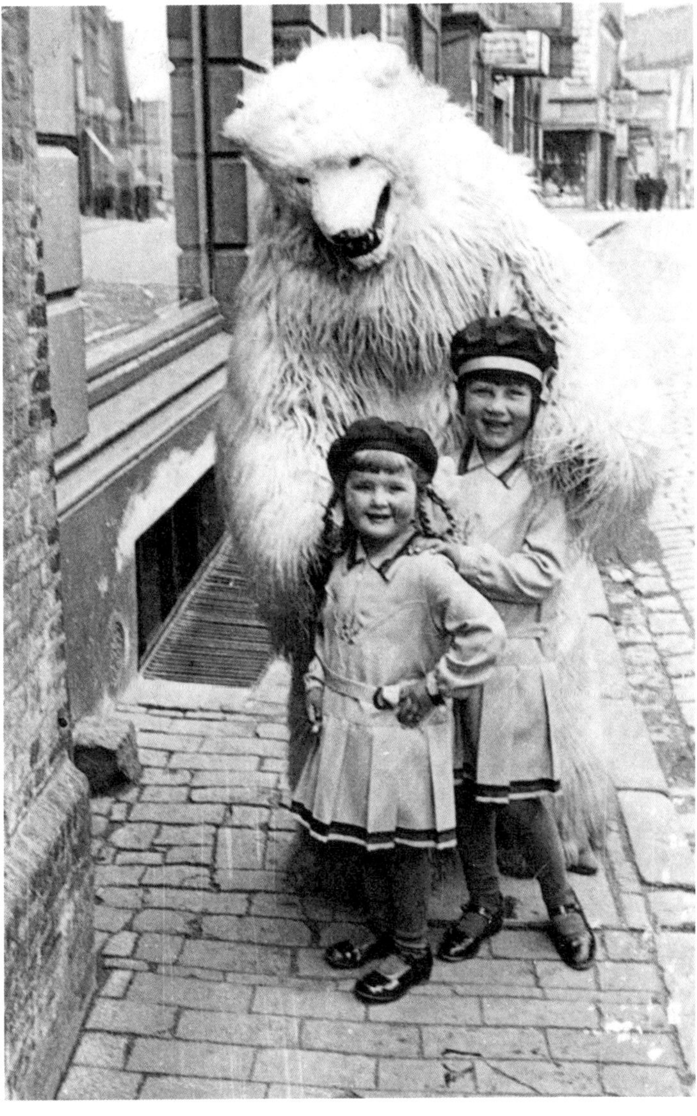

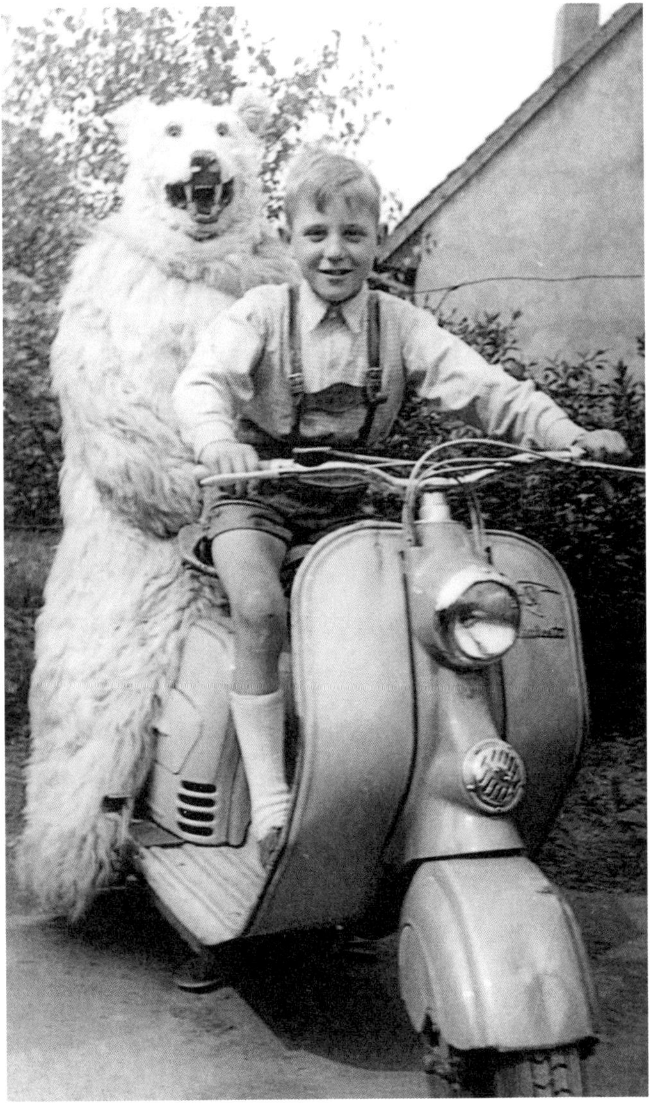

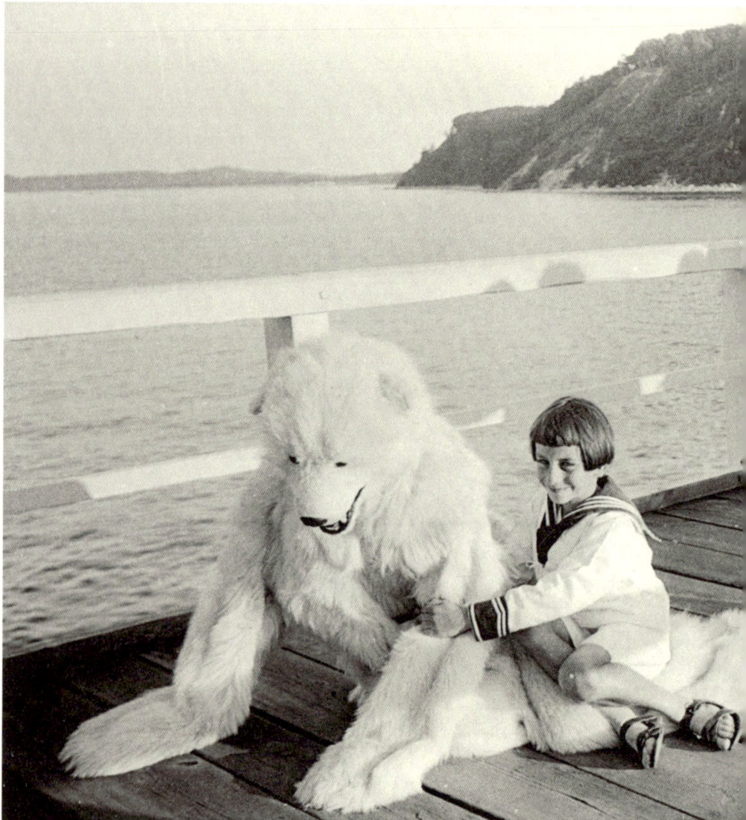

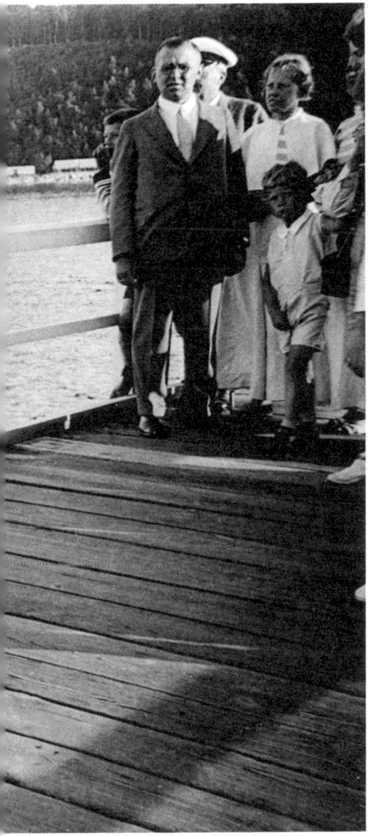

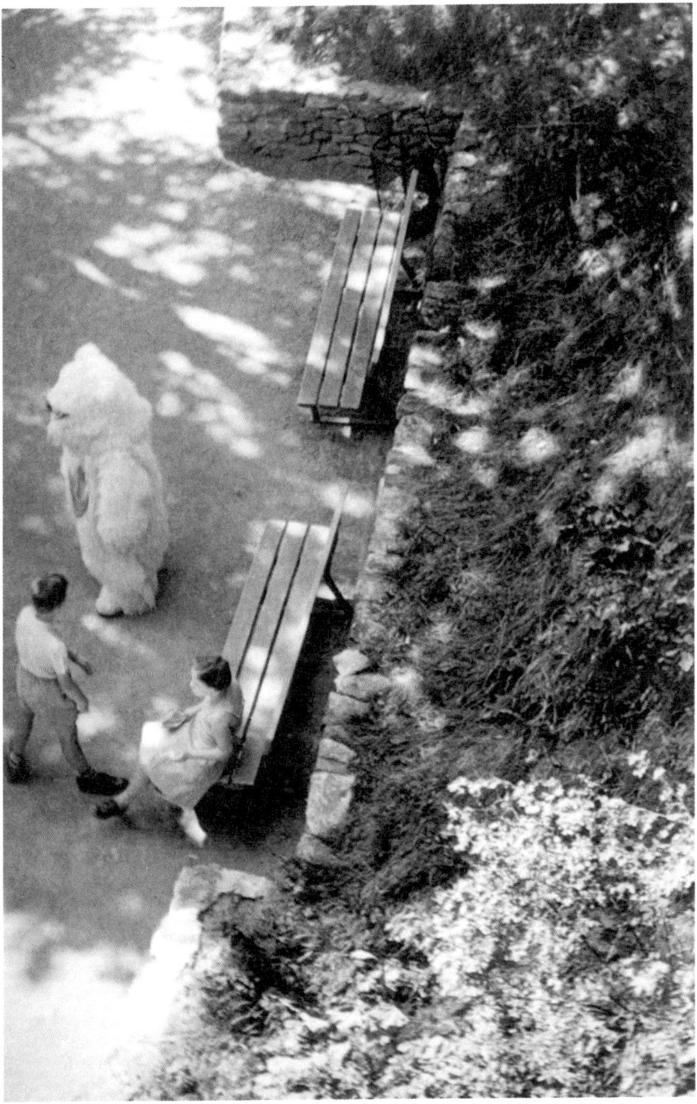

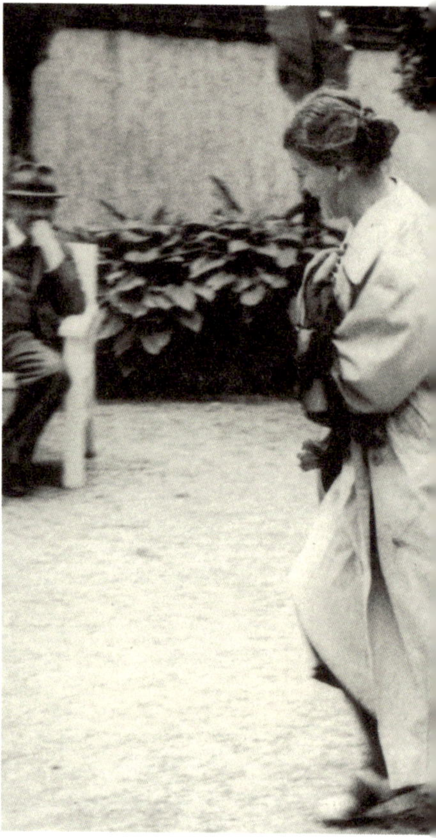

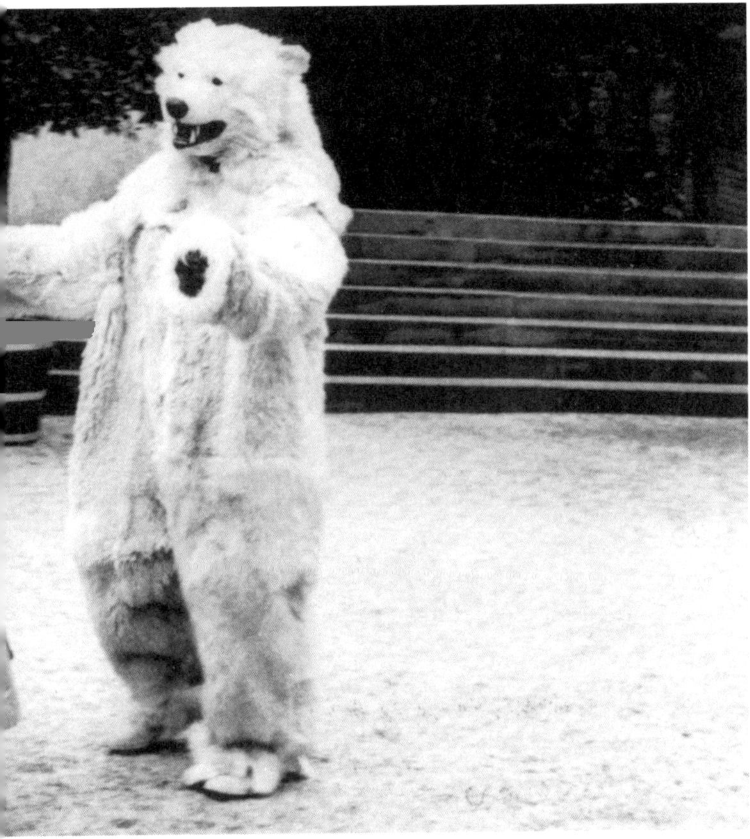

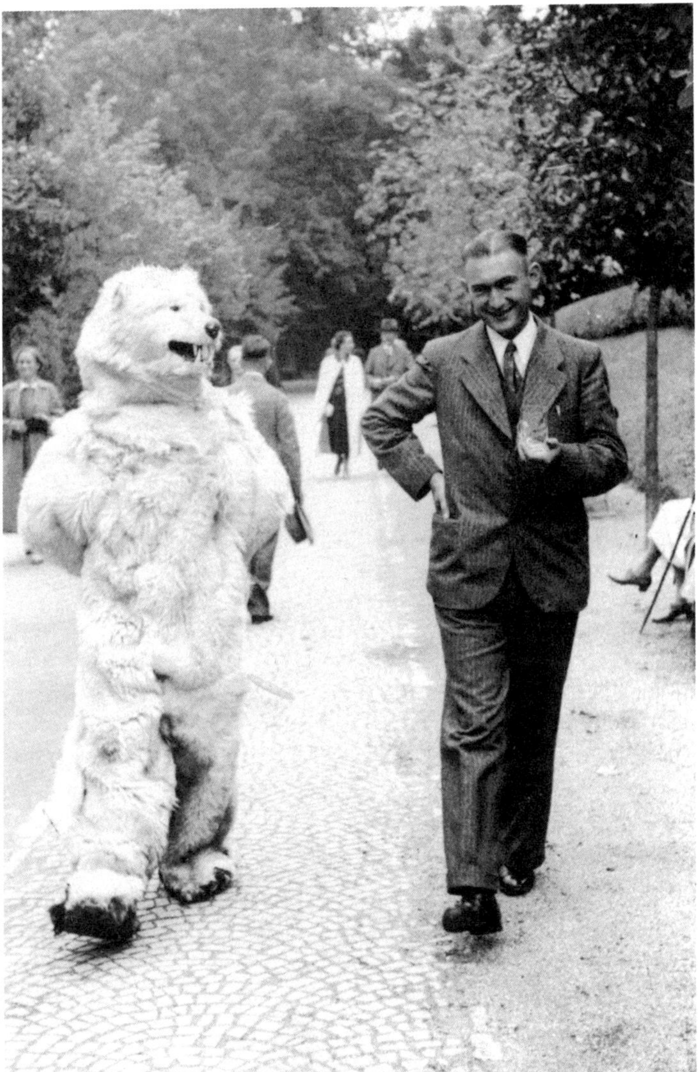

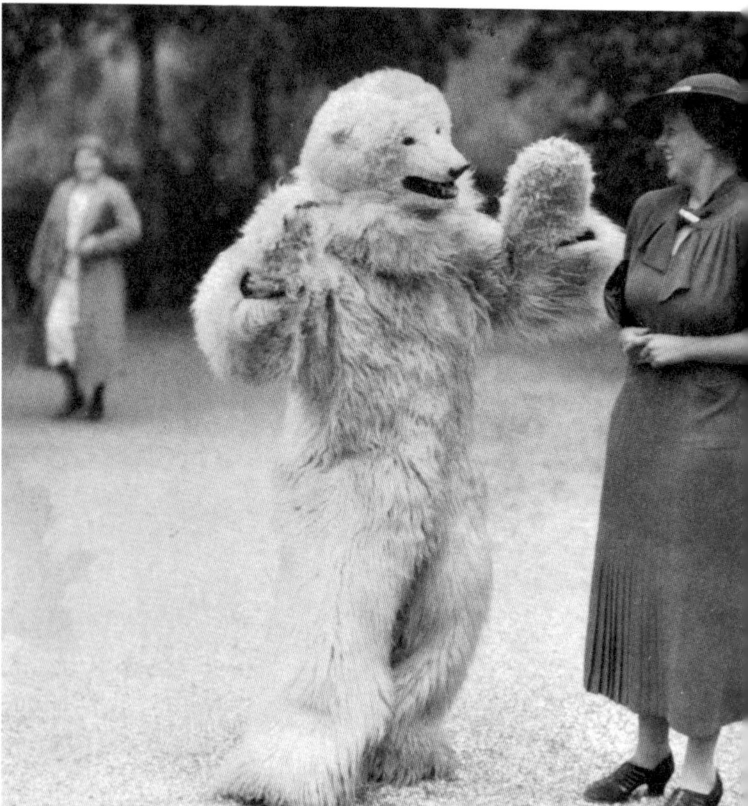

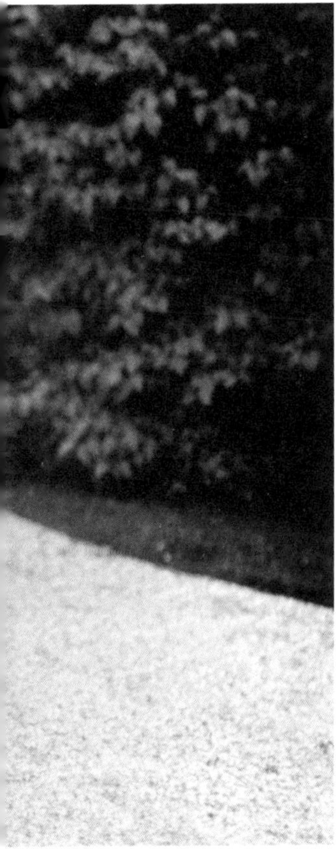

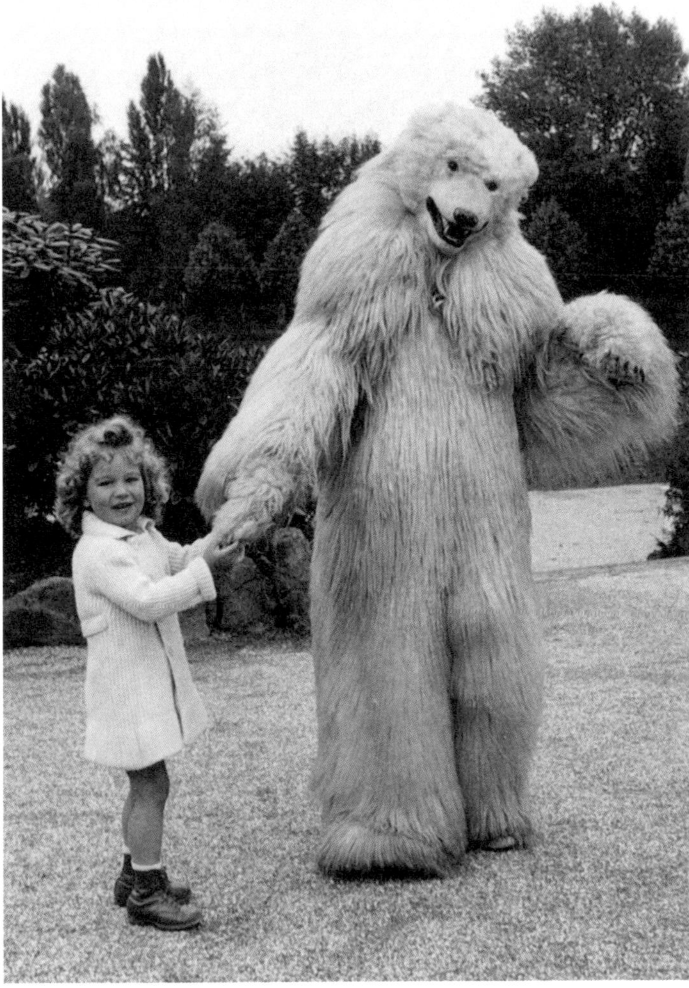

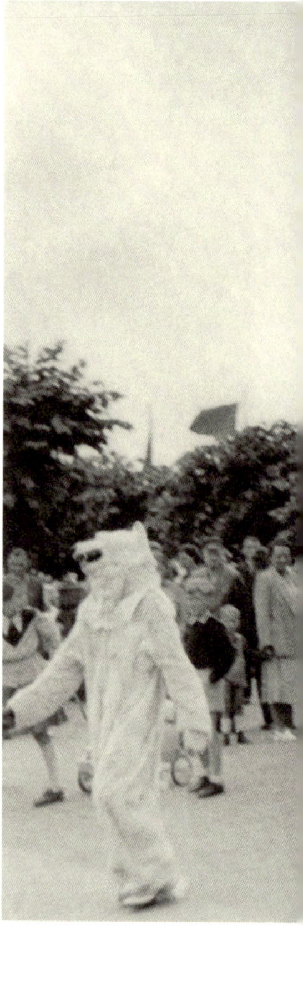

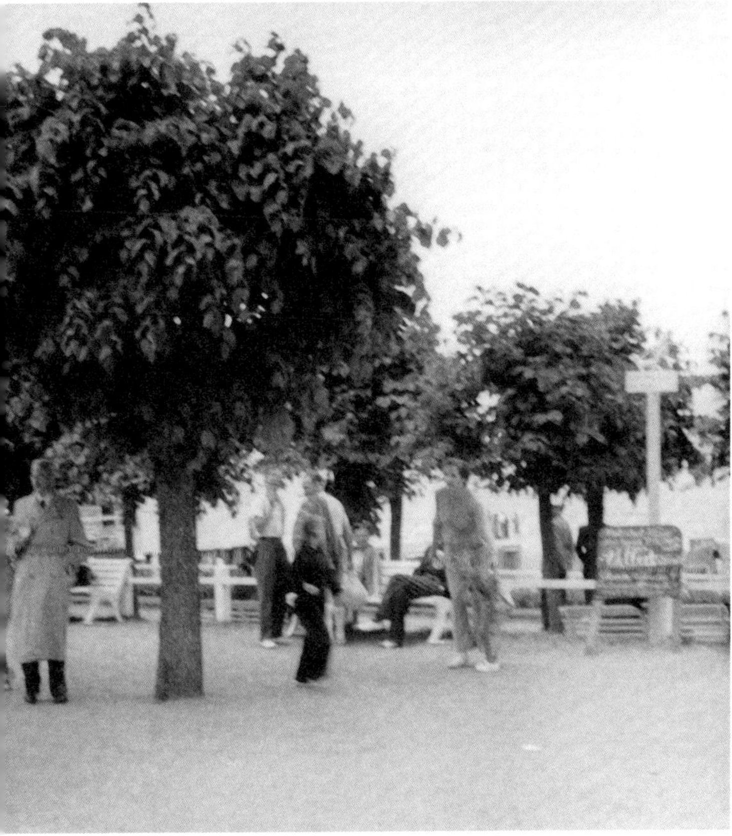

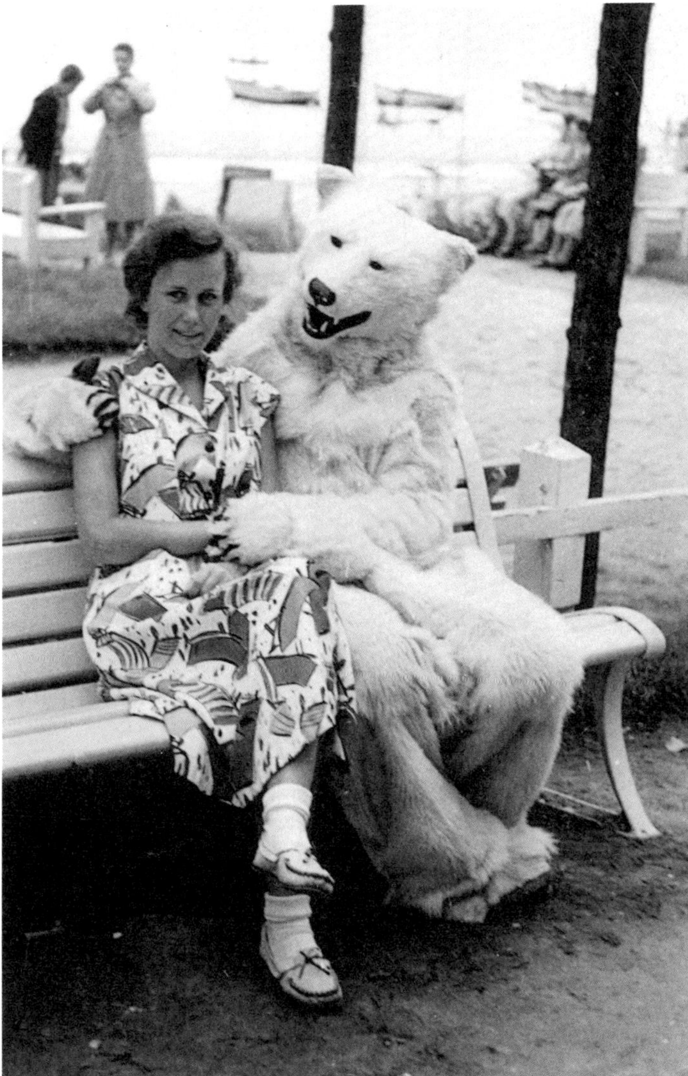

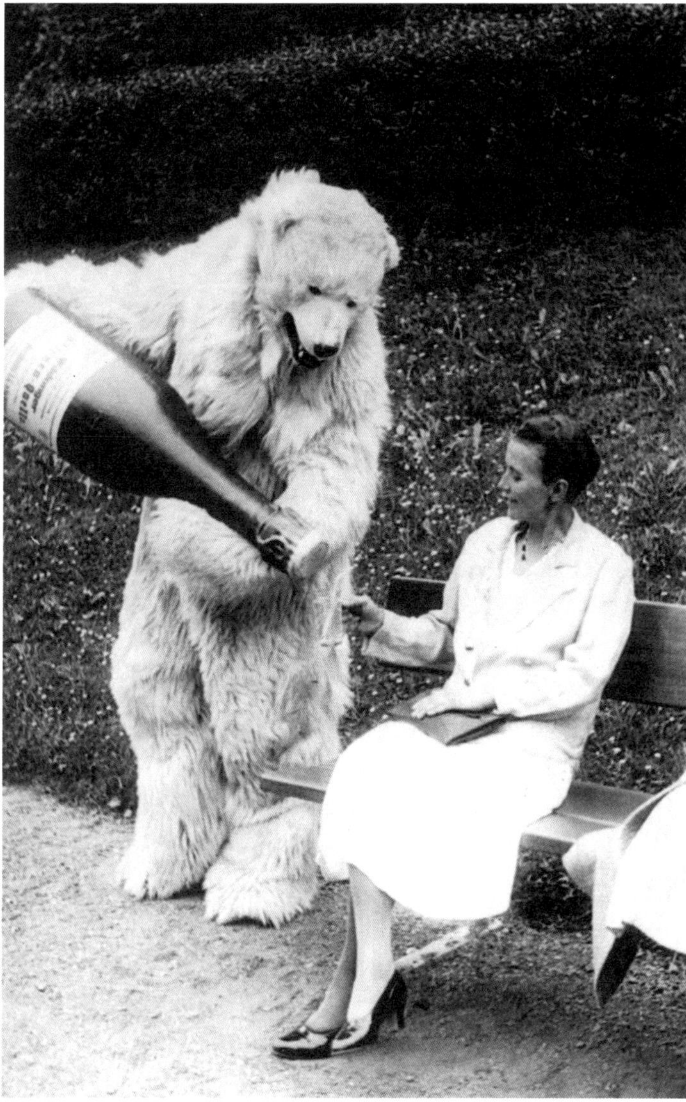

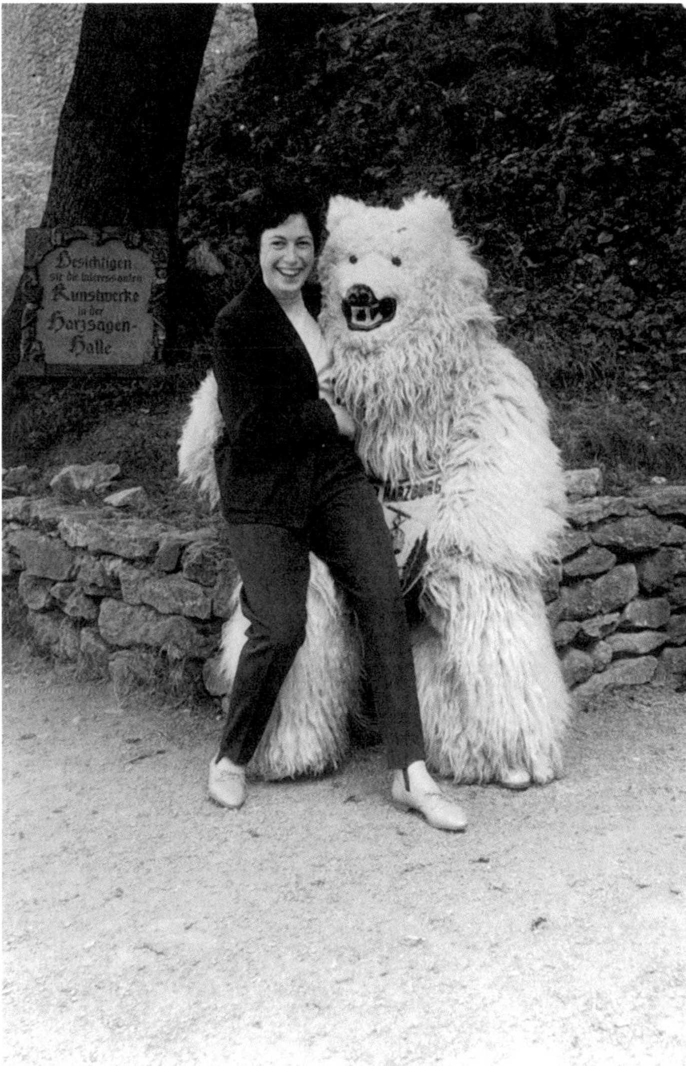
Besichtigen
Kunstwerke
in der
Harzsagen-
Halle

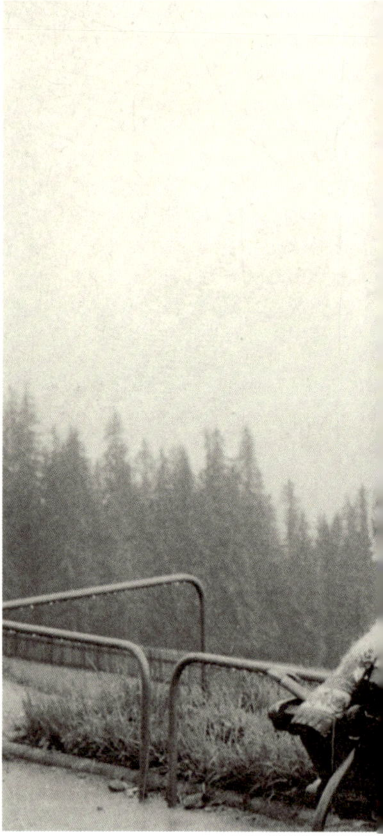

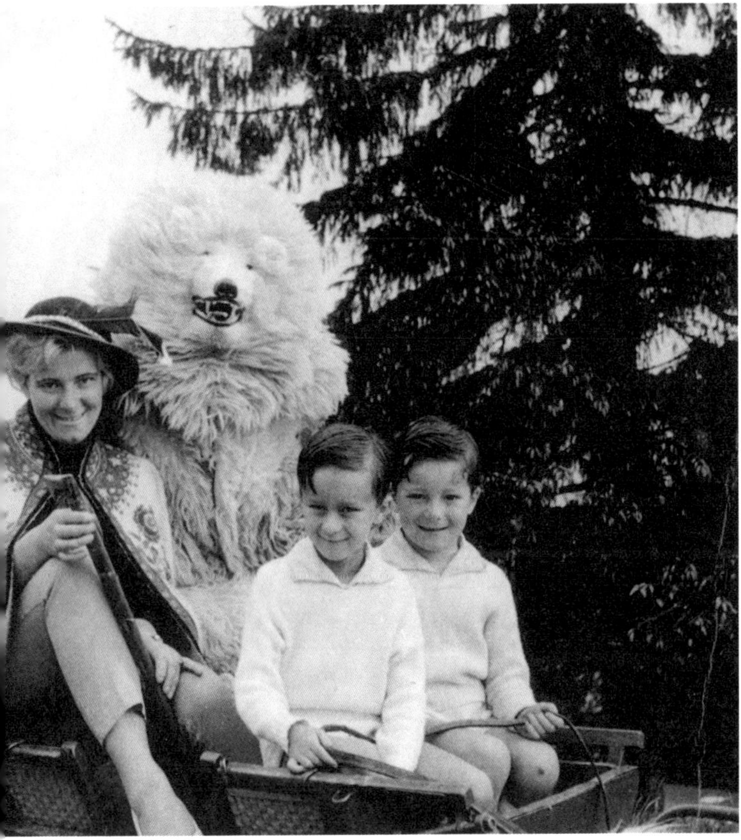

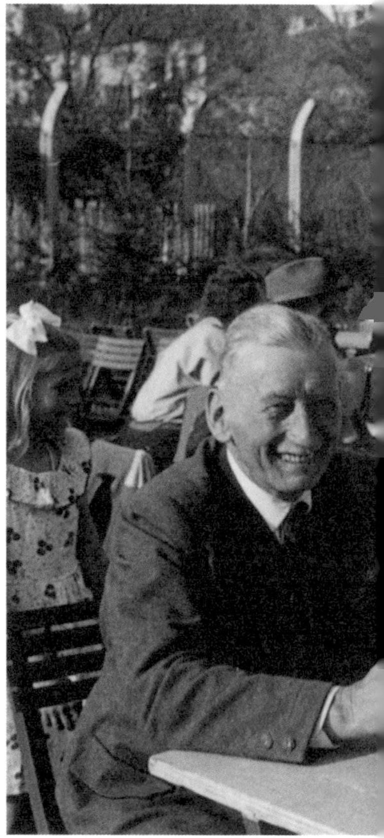

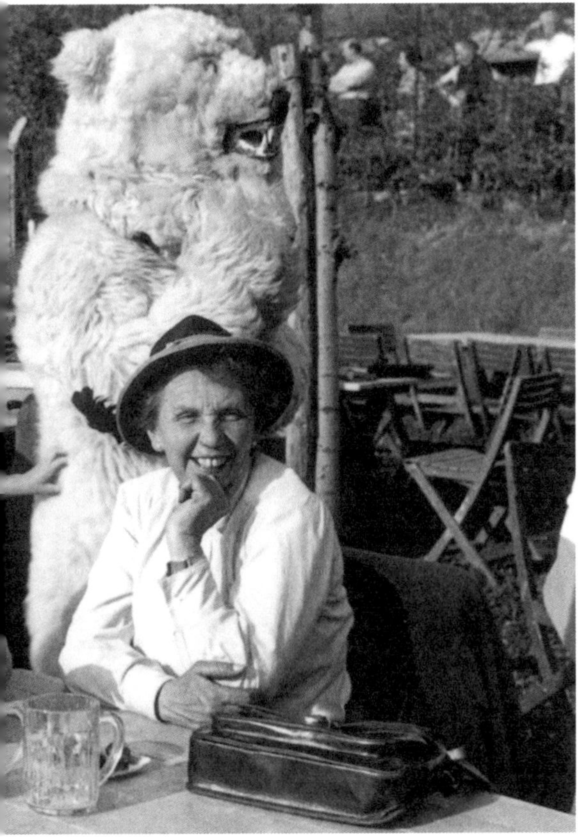

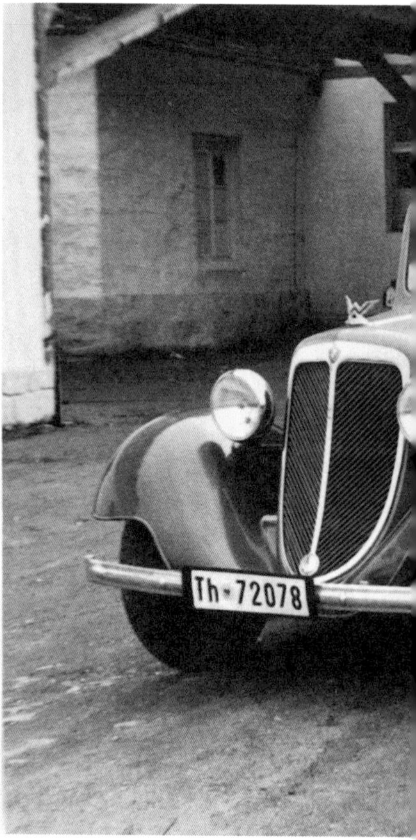
Th-72078

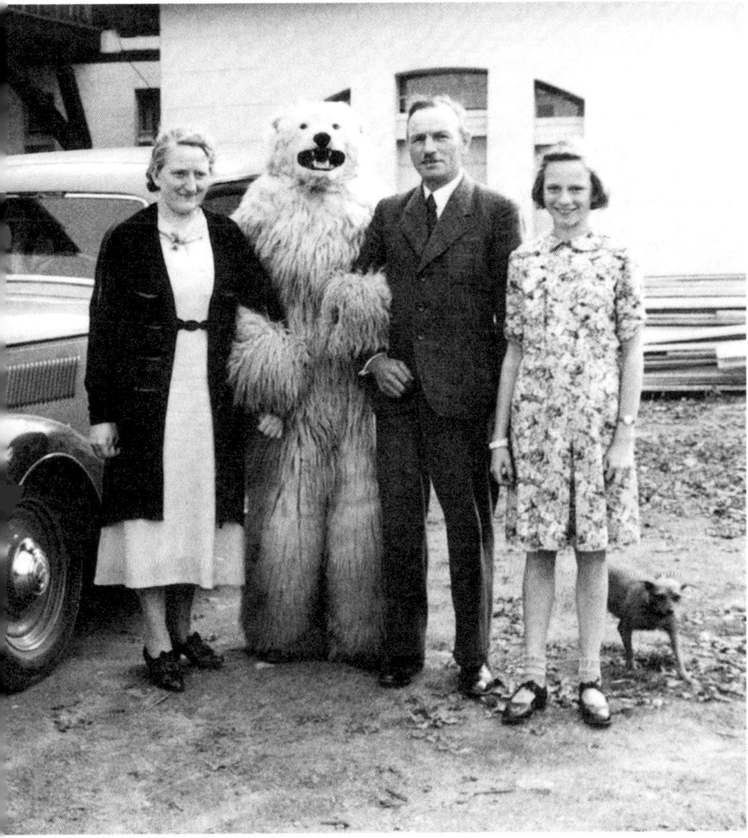

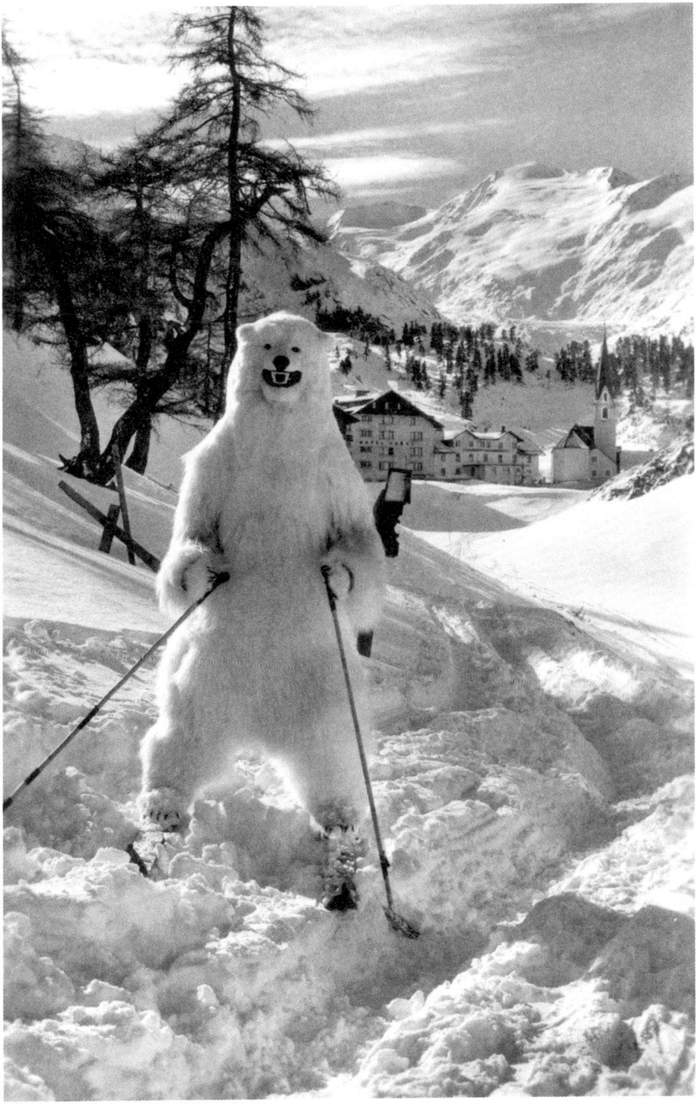

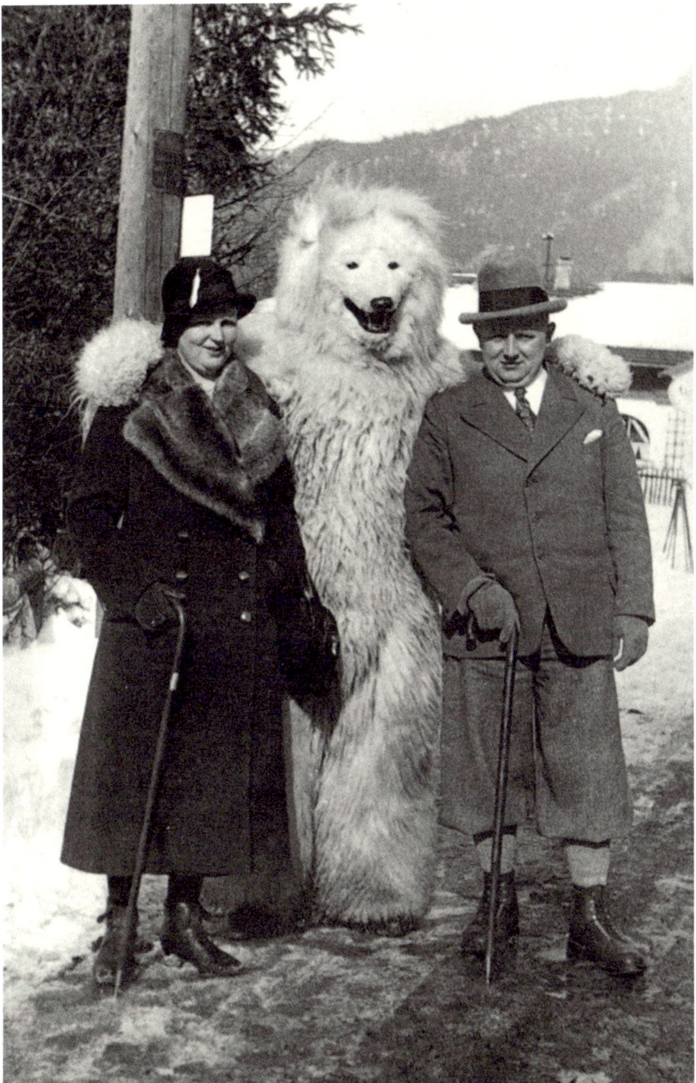

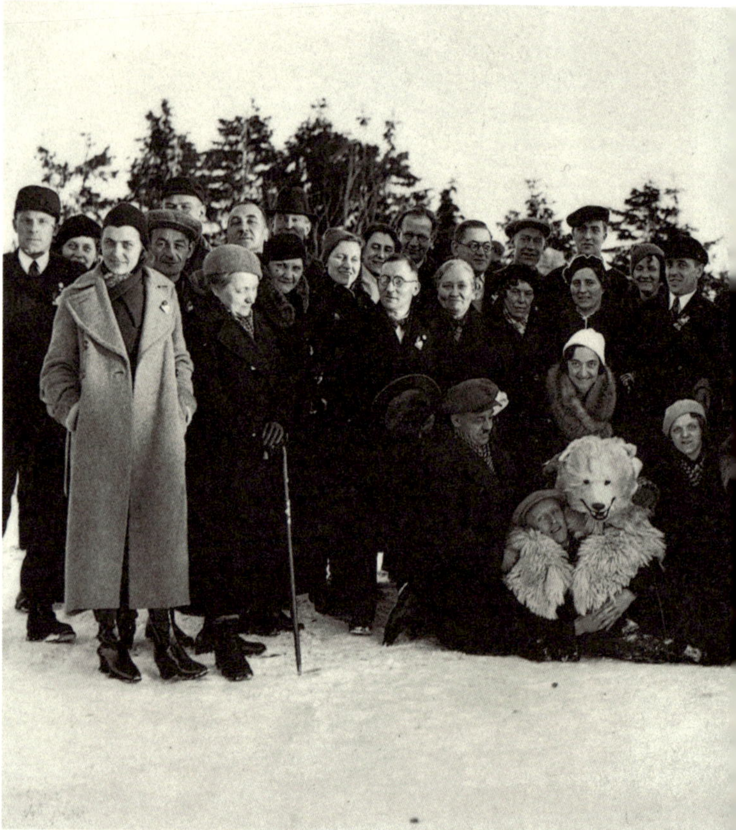

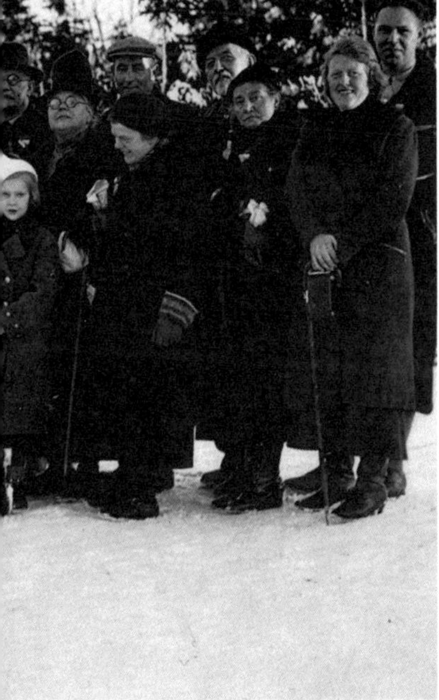

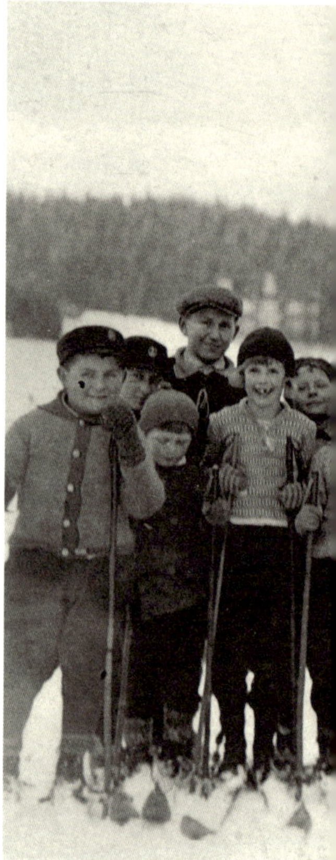

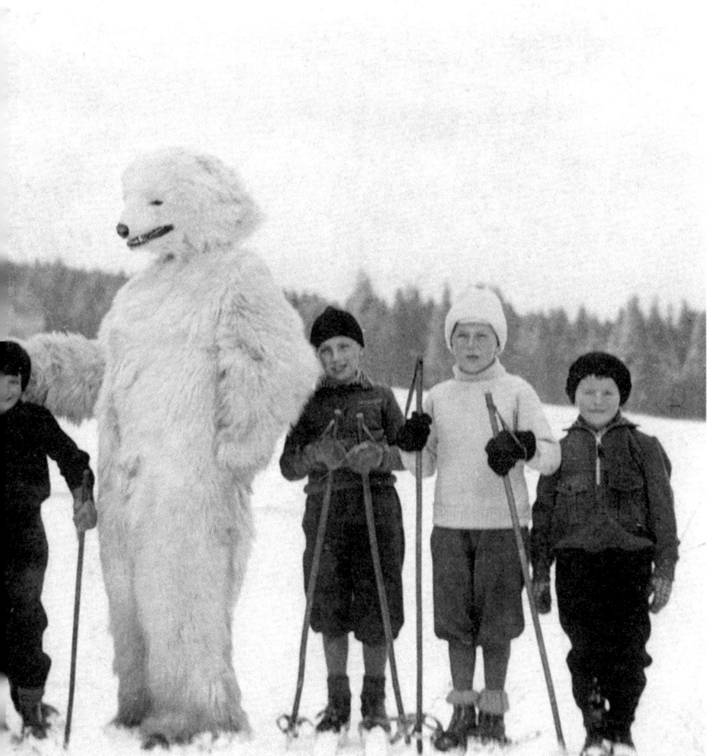

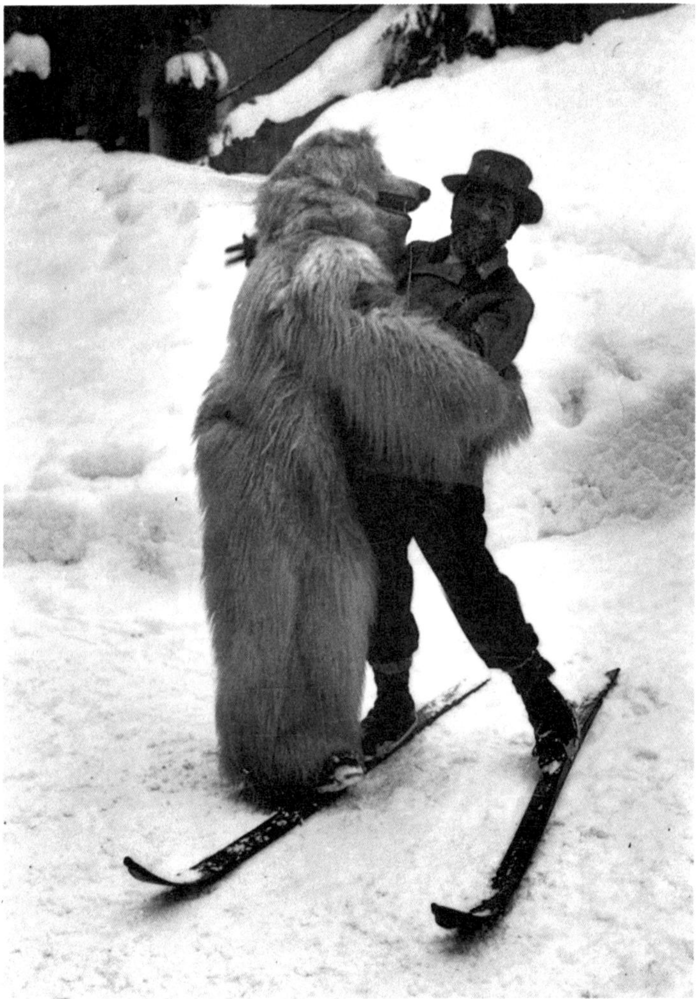

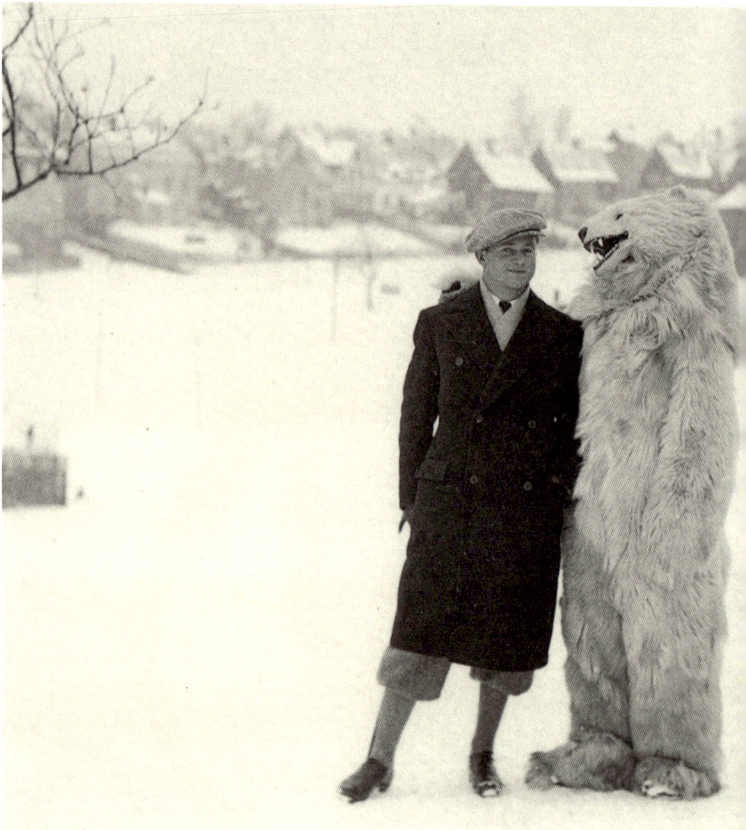

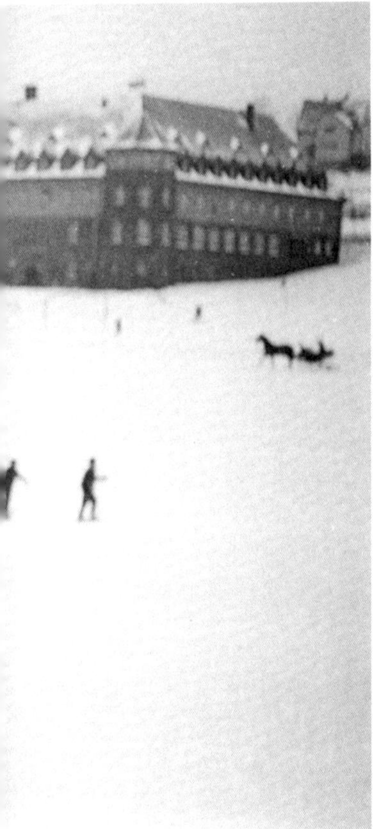

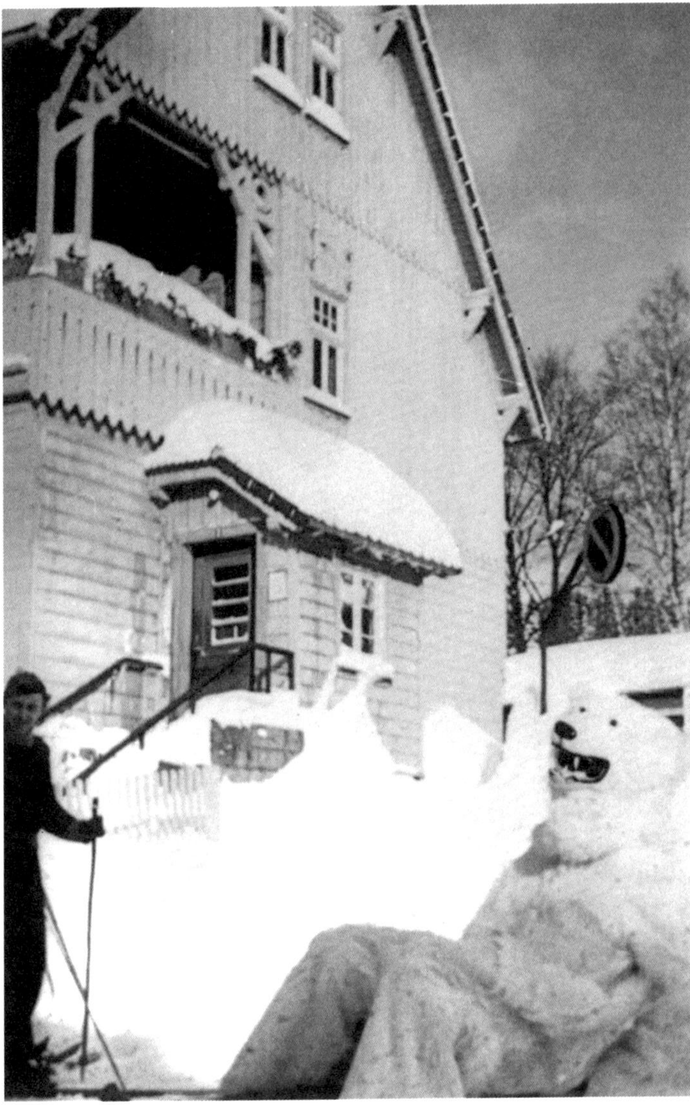

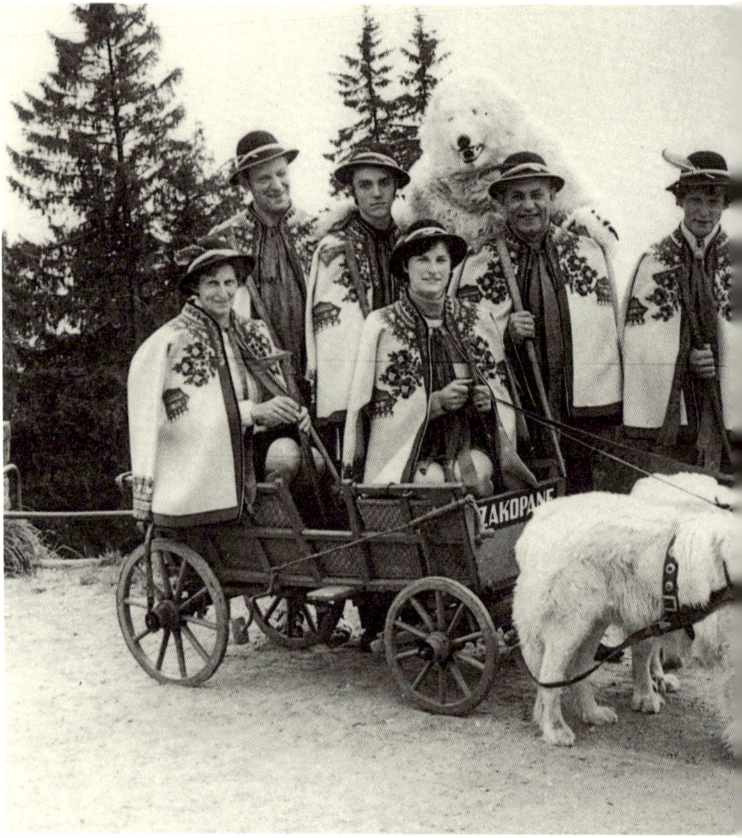
ZAKOPANE

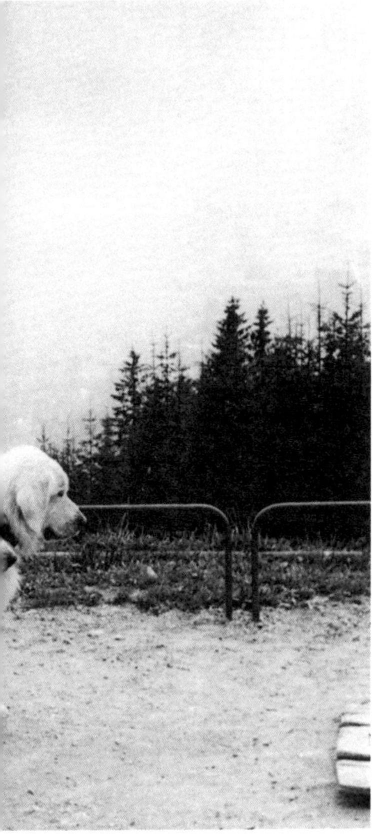

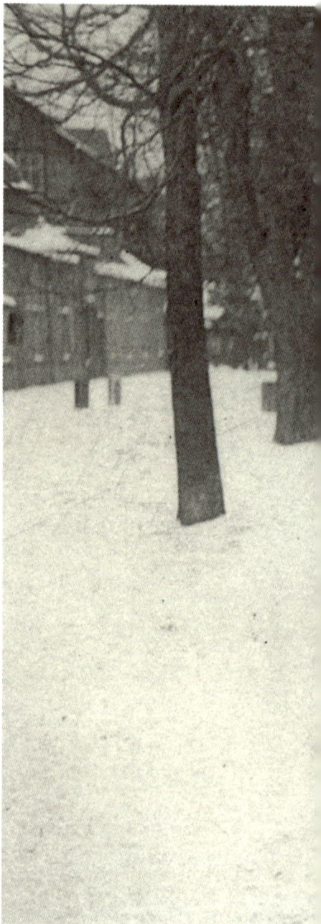

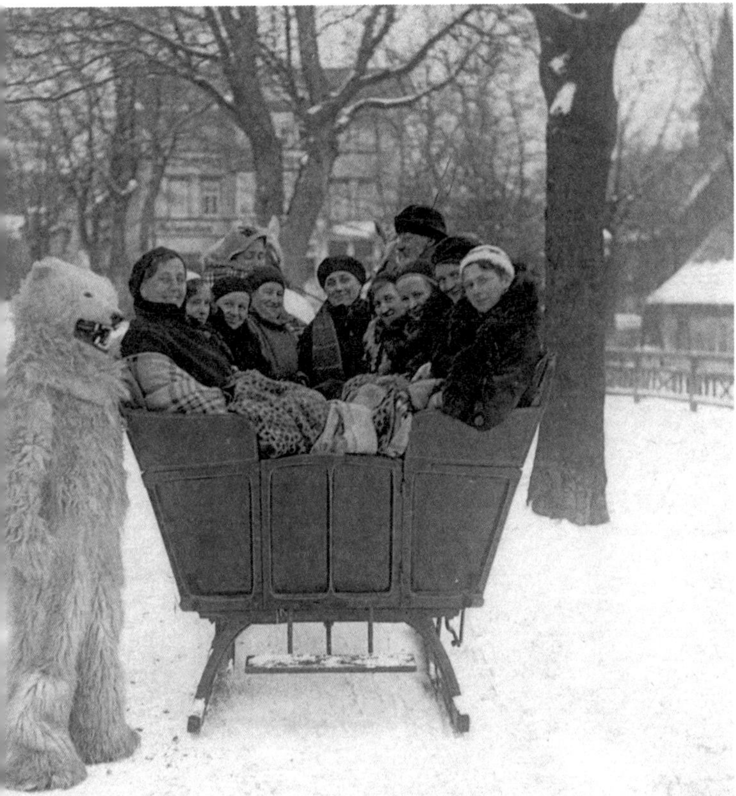

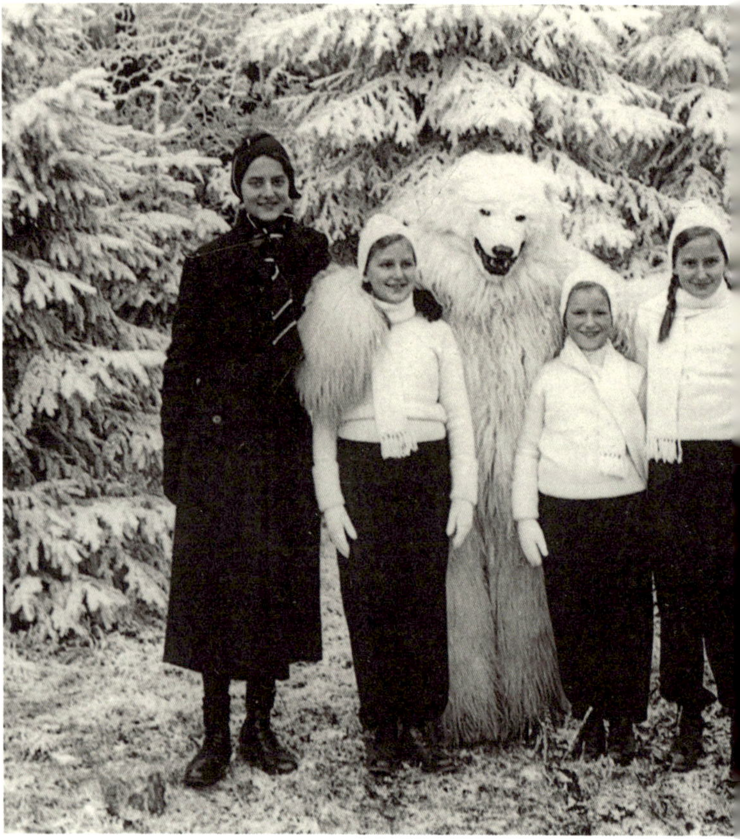

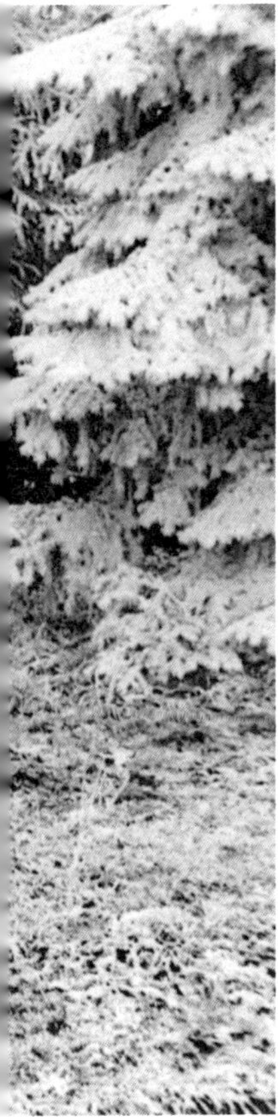

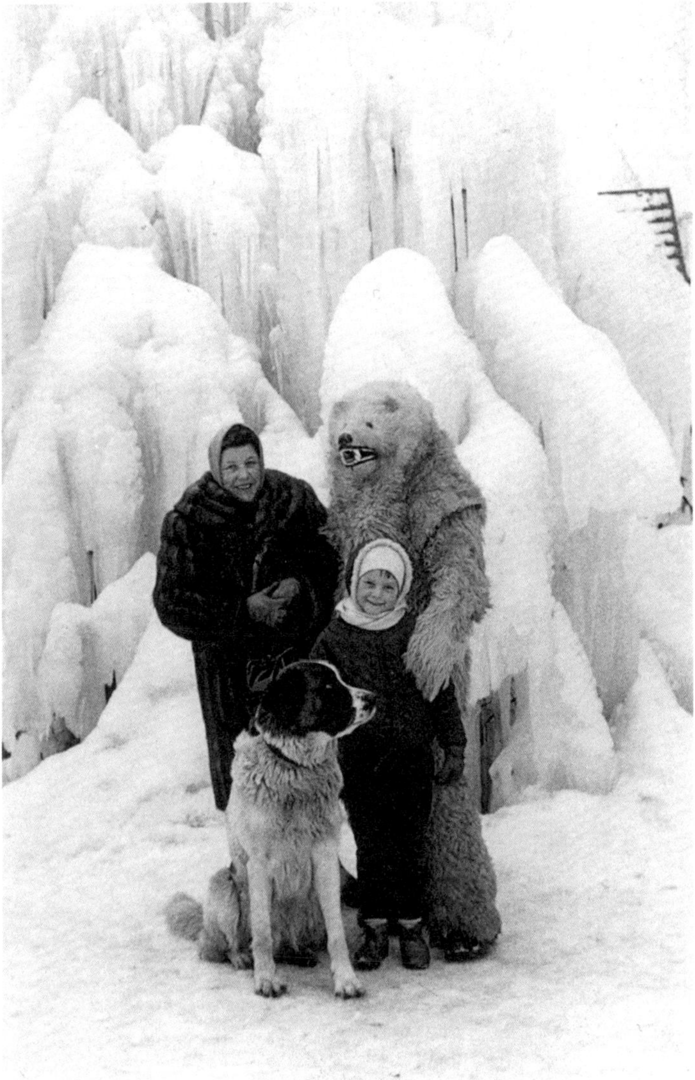

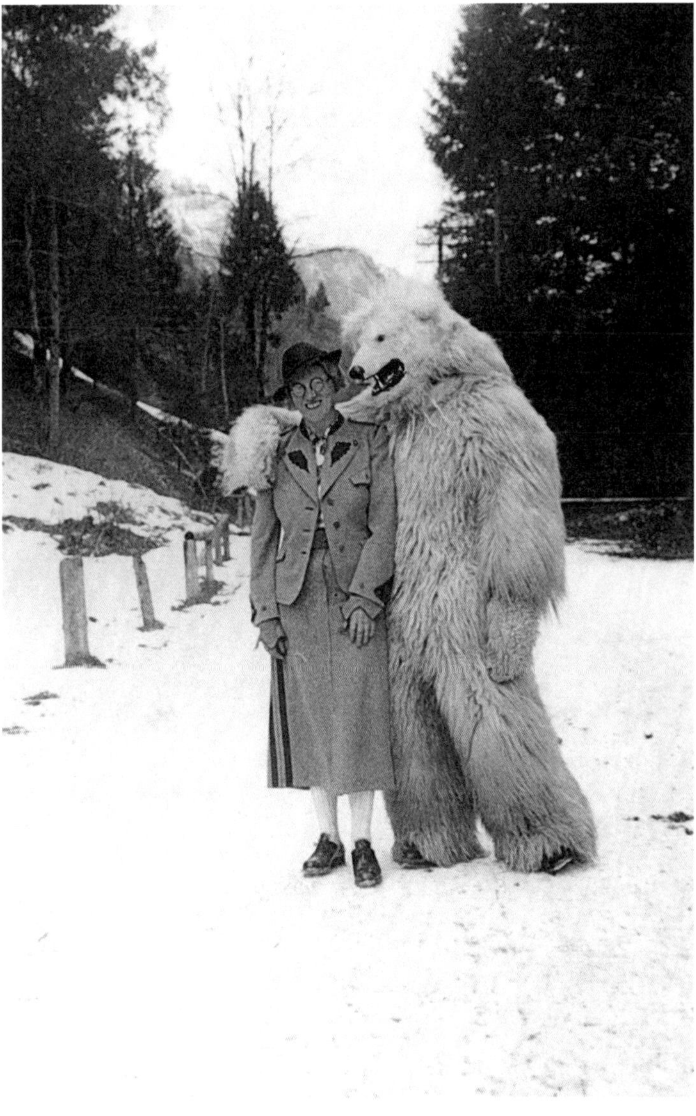

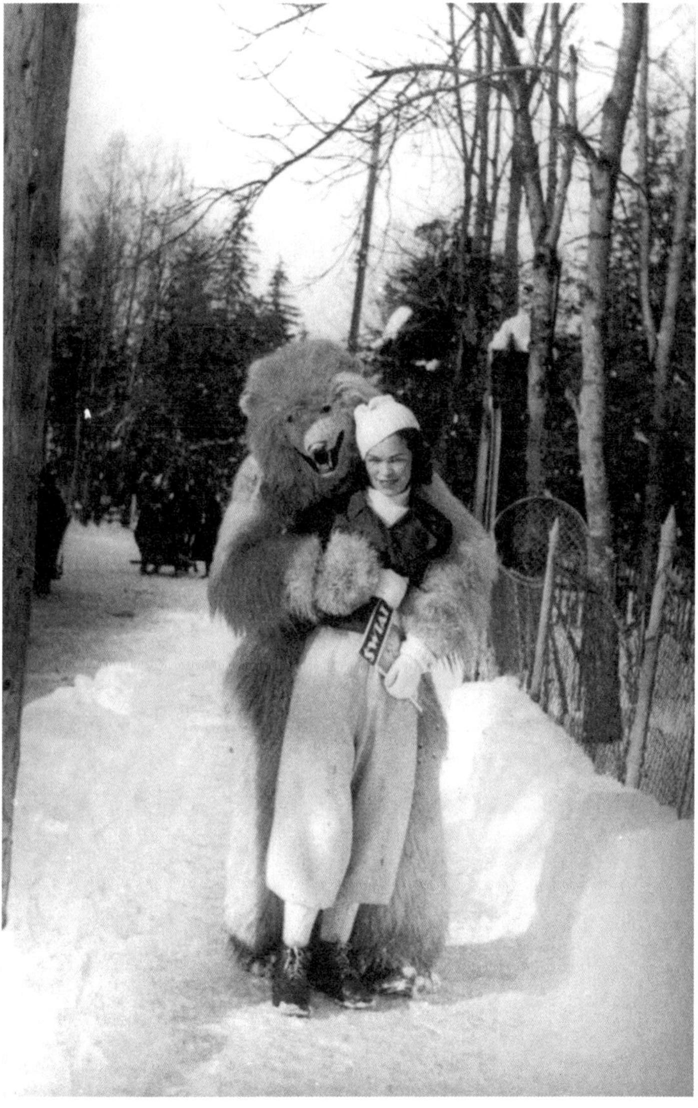

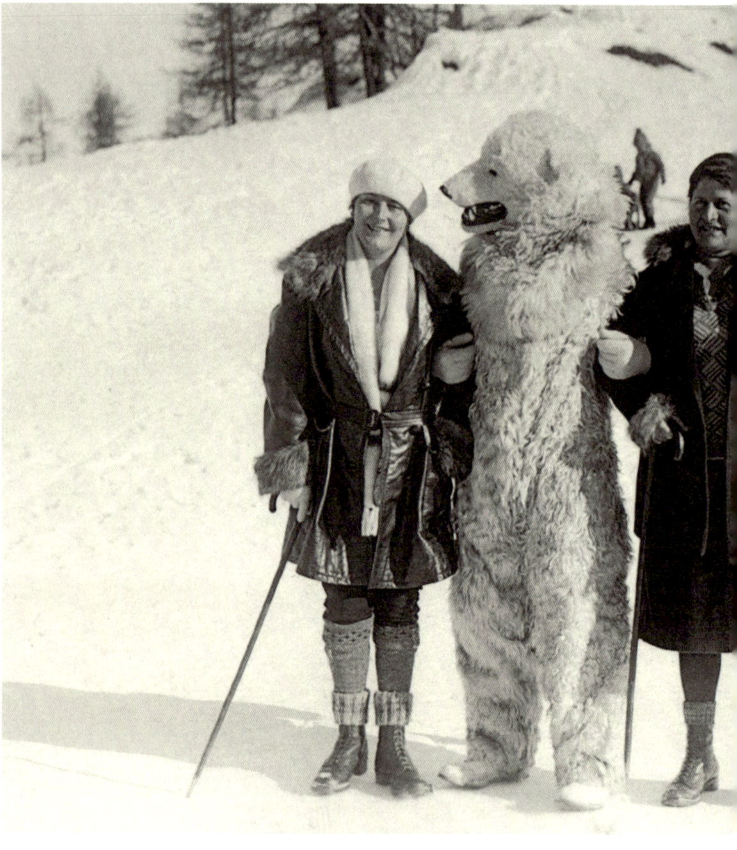

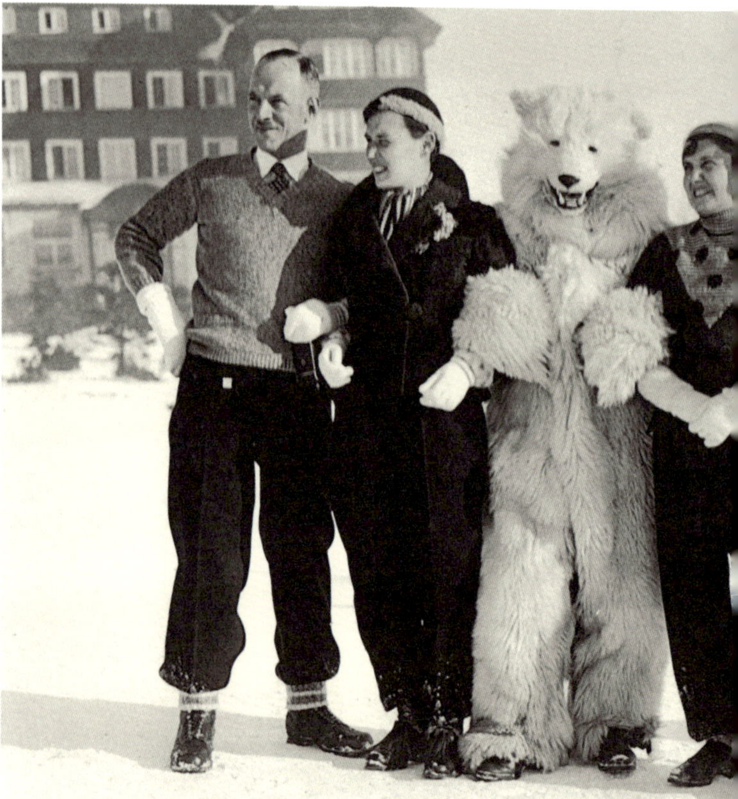

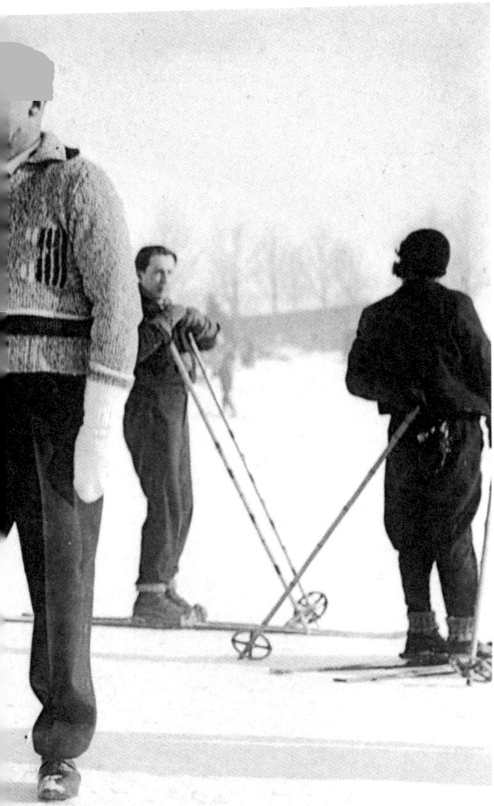

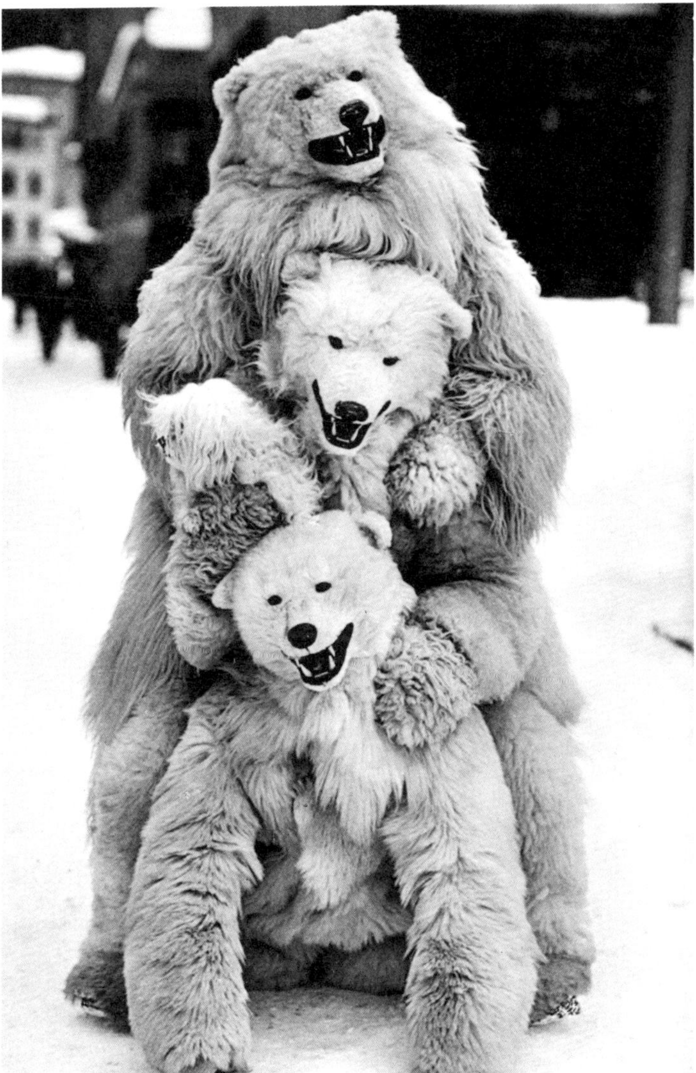

I dedicate this book to the people who wore these costumes to pose for photographs in cold and hot weather and to all those who supported me along the road to this book.

Jochen Raiss

For three decades, Jochen Raiß of Hamburg has been rummaging through flea markets and second-hand bookstores collecting historical amateur photographs, which he presents on his website: imperfekt.photography.

The journalist Norbert Thomma lives in Berlin, rides a bicycle, and speaks to people all over the world; he visited the polar bear Knut back in the day but did not interview him. The funniest polar bear of all times: in the Singapore Zoo.

MIX
Paper from responsible sources
FSC® C015829

Project management:
Richard Viktor Hagemann

Translations:
Steven Lindberg

Copyediting:
Aaron Bogart

Graphic design:
Tanja Pöpping, Köln

Cover design:
Sofarobotnik, München

Production:
Stefanie Kruszyk

Reproductions:
Jan Scheffler, prints professional

Paper:
Salzer Touch White, 120 g/m²

Printing and Production:
Printer Trento S.r.l.

Printed in Italy

Published by
Hatje Cantz Verlag GmbH
Mommsenstraße 27
10629 Berlin
www.hatjecantz.de
A Ganske Publishing Group compan

ISBN 978-3-7757- 4599-4
ISBN 978-3-7757-4597-0
(Eisbären German edition)